Story Copyright © 2021 by: Mike Fiorito
Copy Editor: Tiziano Thomas Dossena
Cover Design and Interior Layout: Dominic A. Campanile
On the front cover: **Sleeping with Fishes** (acrylic and digital) by Pat Singer

ISBN: 978-1-948651-26-4
Library of Congress Control Number: 2021911331
Published by: Idea Press (*an imprint of Idea Graphics, LLC*) — Florida, USA
www.ideapress-usa.com
Administrative Office, Florida, USA • email: ideapress33@gmail.com
Editorial Office, New York, USA • editoreusa@gmail.com

Printed in the USA - 1ˢᵗ Edition, July 2021

MIKE FIORITO

This book is dedicated to all marginalized people
who face discrimination and exclusion.

Acknowledgements

First, I would like to thank Marianne Leone, Susan Caperna Llyod, Christina Marrocco, and Karen Tintori for their support and encouragement. I owe an enormous debt of gratitude to Angela Welch, Bill Bernthal, and Susan Kaessinger for their detailed and constructive inputs. I am very grateful to Charlie Diliberti for reviewing the Sicilian language sections in the book. A great bow of thankfulness to Tiziano for his expert edits and reviews, especially correcting my use of Italian and Sicilian. And thank you to Michelle Messina Reale for creating a thriving community of Italian American writers and thinkers who are forging a new vision.

Foreword

BY: MICHELLE MESSINA REALE,
Author of *Seasons of Subtraction* and *Blood Memory*

We all have a different way of being in the world. No matter which way we were raised, we are free to change things up, starting in young adulthood as we begin our independent relationship with the world around us and the world within us. Today's generation call that "adulting." To most of us, it is just the experience of *becoming an adult*, reaching an age of awareness and crystallized thinking as we go forward with a bit of experience in the form of how we were brought up, and decide how much of that we want to bring along with us. Most Italian Americans carry forth those ways, ways of our parents and their parents before them that form the bedrock of who we are. I once had a friend marvel that he'd not ever seen a culture as proud to be who they were, as Italian Americans are. I'd never thought of it that way, but I think it is true. While we are by no means monolithic, we carry startling similarities no matter where in the United States we were raised. Those similarities form an unofficial kinship, a brotherhood, a sisterhood, a particular belonging that is a profound comfort in an increasingly alienated world and one which enforces a pervasive feeling of being unaffiliated, rooted in nothing. But this is not the Italian American experience.

In these essays, Fiorito gets up close and personal. While his affection for his culture is evident, he is unafraid of interrogating aspects that he does not understand, as well as pointing out peculiarities and inconsistencies. All of these things are part of the collective Italian American experience, and Fiorito lays them out with warmth, humor and an evident and heartwarming *admiration*. These essays bear witness to a distinct culture rooted firmly in American culture. Italian Americans have been able to successfully, and with much joy, blend the very best of both worlds, at times fraught and at times humorous, but always with great heart.

I was so fortunate to meet Mike when I began *Ovunque Siamo*, an online journal to curate the writing of Italian Americans. His submissions were whimsical, wildly creative, inventive and full of love. He cares about people and he cares about culture. He comes from probably the most well-presented Italian American experience in the United States—that of the New York Italian American. His voice is unique, his insight sharp, his humor extraordinarily delightful. Whether he is writing about family, pastries, language, childhood, neighborhoods, he does so with deep respect and curiosity. Culture is important and testifying to it and curating it even more so. Mike Fiorito is one of the premier voices writing about the Italian American experience in the United States today, giving us contributions that will be read generations from now. We are so grateful to him and to his extraordinary talents. *Evviva la cultura!*

Table of Contents

1

My Mother is Not Italian

"When we were kids, we never felt Italian," says my mother to my wife, Arielle. "We were American," she adds.

My eighty-six-year-old mom is now homebound. She's fallen a few times, broken a vertebra and recently her hip too. We're visiting her on a Saturday night. Of course, we bring food and wine.

My mother grew up on the Lower East Side in the '30s and '40s. The Elizabeth Street of her youth is thronged with Russians, Poles, Italians, and Jews from all over Europe. Her parents are Sicilians and they both spoke the Sicilian dialect.

"My parents never spoke Sicilian in front of us," she says, sternly.

"I remember them speaking Sicilian," I say.

"They were *my* parents; don't you think I'd remember?" she adds, raising her voice, looking over at Arielle. My mother is teasing, but Arielle doesn't know what to think, even though she's seen this before. My mother talks as if I'm making all of this up.

"They spoke Sicilian to me," I reply defiantly. When my mom raises her voice, it makes it hard for me to think, like I'm caught in a windstorm trying to open an umbrella. Even though I know she's needling. To counter her intensity, I've learned to bark back a little. To stand my ground.

All joking aside, the fact is my mother is tough. This toughness is in our lineage. We Southern Italians came to this country with nothing. We came only with our bodies. We were mocked, treated poorly. Since the dawn of cinema, we've been portrayed—for the entire world to see—as tough goons or thugs (even until today). To protect ourselves, we reinforce our on-screen image. But we're not without a sense of humor. *You talking to me?* We argue, sometimes loudly, often with our hands. To the outside world it can be hard to tell where our rage ends, and our joking begins. *Do I amuse you; do I make you laugh?* The tradition continues when my brother and I grapple at my mom's house on holidays. *You never knocked me down, Ray!* My mother still calling us jerks.

Then I remember.

"When I was studying Italian in high school, I spoke to them, practicing what I was learning. Grandma would speak back, and I would stare blankly at her. Grandpa would make fun of me. *Michele Lu Scupaturi Se Caga Li Pantaloni.* Michael the sweeper shits in his pants."

"They never spoke Italian to me."

Now I laugh at her a little. Arielle chuckles, too. Even my mom acknowledges the absurdity of this exchange. There's a bit of performance in it all. Like an opera.

"I asked them to teach me," I say. It's coming back to me now in detail. "When I spoke Italian to Grandpa, he spoke Sicilian back to me, but I could never understand him." *Mancia cava* (shortened version of *Mancia comu 'n cavaddu).* He eats like a horse. Words truncated, or just completely different. The grammar is so mangled I can't decipher the meanings.

My mother is still shaking her head no.

While my mother often gives me a hard time, she's sweet and gentle to Arielle. My mother loves her; Arielle can do no wrong. Except for the time Arielle tells my mother that she made meatballs with carrots and peas so our son Travis would eat more vegetables.

"You did what?" I hear my mother's voice explode over the phone. I'm sitting next to Arielle on the couch.

I can see Arielle is in shock now. She looks over at me and shrugs her shoulders. My mother's attack catches her off guard.

"He's not eating enough vegetables," Arielle answers, girding herself for my mother's assault. I'm enjoying this because Arielle always gets the *royal* treatment. Now she's getting yelled at by my mom. Like she's the one in trouble. It's her turn to decipher the ancient codes of joking and antagonism, this time being in the center of the storm.

"I've never heard of anyone putting vegetables in meatballs."

Arielle's eyes plead with me to assist, as I laugh.

Now I hear my mother give her the meatball recipe. How to make the sauce, letting the sauce cook with pork and sausages. Bones, if you can get them. Let the meat cook with the sauce to give it flavor.

When learning Sicilian from my grandparents, I recall specific phrases and words.

"We say *patri* for father," my grandmother says. And *bedda* for beautiful. "You couldn't understand our language," she remarks. "We don't speak the right way." I think to myself, *then how come you understand it?*

I have no idea why the language they speak is so different from the language I'm learning in school. It's frustrating. I don't yet know the history behind all of this. I want to study something I can use.

"I never heard them speaking Sicilian," my mother says again, refusing to give in. This can't even be true. Now that she's had a few glasses of wine, she repeats herself. Each repetition a notch more intense.

I find all this ironic, especially since, long ago, as a student, I felt strangled by our Italian-ness. My brother and my friends from college come over to our house to meet our family, or to visit. These friends are from other parts of the country, other countries.

"He likes the sauce," my mother says, referring to Mark, my brother's roommate at Columbia University. Mark is from Blacksburg, Virginia.

"Do you want some more?" my mother asks, forking a piece of pork.

"Yes, and some noodles," he says.

"You mean *macaroni*," she replies. They claw their Italian-ness back with the words, though they themselves aren't aware of it.

"Yes, macaroni," repeats Mark, looking at us for approval. My brother and I smirk.

My parents watch Mark eat.

He cleans his plate with a piece of bread, mimicking my brother.

"You don't want no more?" asks my father. They will keep feeding him until he begs them to stop. Trying to be polite, he keeps accepting their offers. This is an ancient form of Southern Italian generosity. Your generosity must outpace your means. And you can never take anything. If my grandparents or uncles offer us money, I look at my parents for approval. If they nod *yes,* I take the money. They never nod no, but I never take without their approval. Taking is indiscrete.

"They like to come back to have a home-cooked meal," says my father after Mark leaves. While that may be true, I know that visitors are intrigued by our family, our home. It's very New York City Italian. The hand gestures. Each of us seeming to yell at the other. Speaking an English that's different from theirs. "They don't do that no more." Or "Oh my God, he eats like a *gavone.*" They say words like *manicot* and *ricot,* making Mark giggle. It sounds strange. He's not mocking our family. He's seeing real-life examples of people he's only seen on television. People like Rocky, or Travolta from *Saturday Night Fever.* Or Mona Lisa Vito from *My Cousin Vinny.* Just like if I went to Virginia and ate at Mark's house, hearing their local language with local color, using a vocabulary that wouldn't be familiar to me, except for what I've seen on television or in the movies.

And I understand why my mother wants to be American. Being different is hard. Standing out is scary. During the turn of the century, as Southern Italians immigrate in droves to America, they are called *cafones* by Northern Italians. *Cafone* means pig in English, but it's also akin to the word hillbilly. The word *cafone* becomes *gavone* in dialect.

Gavone is said often in our home all my life. Even until today. Most of us don't know the history of our own words.

My grandparents want their children to speak English. In their view, they speak English and Italian poorly. They don't want their children to be confused by a useless language that only reminds them of the country that exiles them. A country that squeezes the very life out of its poor. So much so that they are willing to flee it to come to a country they don't know that doesn't want them and speaks a language they don't know. Especially back then, as Mussolini's Italy, in league with Hitler, edged the world to war.

Now I am remembering for my mother, for my grandparents. I am remembering for a generation of people kicked in the head by the Southern Italian boot. Giving everyone a generational amnesia.

And I'll start with the words. Word by word I will dig a trench underground, under the earth, under the ocean, back to Sicily. I write down word by word, phrase by phrase. The expressions that I dredge up from what feels like an imaginary past.

The words will lead me back to the source.

2

Italian When We Eat

Sitting in my grandparents' kitchen, eating dinner, we watch the Mike Douglas show. I am twelve years old. Since both of my parents are working, I am at my grandparents' because I am sick.

My grandparents don't eat in the parlor, so they wheel the television on its stand, tilting it toward the kitchen. This is where I learn fragments of Italian, or more specifically, their Sicilian dialect version of Italian, which is quite different.

I write down the words on a piece of paper. *Patri* for *padre, Bedda* for *bella.*

Interestingly though, my grandparents only use Sicilian to speak to each other. They never talk to us in Sicilian.

"It's too hard for you to understand," my grandmother says.

Then, when I start to learn Italian in high school, I practice on my grandfather.

I butcher some words, attempt a hacked sentence.

He laughs.

He then sings *Michele Lu Scupaturi Se Caga Li Pantaloni.* Michael the sweeper shits in his pants.

Seeing the look on my face, my grandfather changes his tone.

"*Ti Vogghiu,*" he says, which I hear as "I want you."

I stare at him, not knowing what he's saying.

"I love you, it means," he says. "What do they teach you in school?"

Apparently, not much. It seems that whatever I learn is only a little bit useful when I try to speak to them. They seem to understand me—sometimes. But mostly I do not understand what they are saying.

The only time my grandparents, and even my own parents, freely speak Italian is when it comes to food. But even then, they use their own words. You have to appreciate how confusing all of this is to a kid's mind.

My grandmother calls pizza *a'pizz*. Instead of just saying *oregano* she rolls her r's, making the word sound exotic.

But then there are all the other words: *mozzarella, pasta e fagioli, ricotta, capicola*, for example. While my mother claims her parents never teach her Sicilian—they want her to be American—she acquires the pronunciation of the food words. Italian food words are safe. Though Americans might look at us funny when we speak Italian, especially Sicilian, they accept the Italian language when it comes to food. Why is this? Italians, especially Southern Italians, are darker, louder, and tougher. Even though we are Christian, by and large, the Catholicism of Southern Italians is more carnal, more pagan, and dramatic; quite different from the Protestant Christianity of America. But Italians ingratiate their way into the hearts of Americans with food: the aromatic smell of garlic, pasta with sauce, lasagna, meatballs, spaghetti and, of course, pizza. Italian foods are now as American as hot dogs and apple pie.

While my family feels comfortable using Italian food words, I later learn that they say them all wrong.

Going to dinner parties with fellow students at college, they say *mozzarella*, and *ricotta*. *Pasta e fagioli* instead of *pasta fazool*. I feel ridiculous saying *ricotta*, so I say *a'regautta*.

I hear laughs from the table.

"What?"

"It's *ricotta*, not *a'regautta*."

More laughs.

"I've used the word all my life, thank you," I say, though I do feel self-conscious now.

"Well, you said it wrong. I guess you Sicilians from Queens didn't learn how to talk the right way."

And of course, to some extent, they are correct. We do not learn how to say the words correctly. Whereas all Italians speak a local dialect, most Southern Italians who immigrate to America speak *only* their local dialects. Owing mostly to their lack of education, Sicilians, like my grandparents, work in labor jobs; their language is crude, grammatically incorrect. When they come to America, they live in enclaves with Italians from the same region. And naturally, in America they take labor jobs, drop out of school early and speak a crude form of English. Of course, this isn't everyone's experience.

Even until today, when I visit my mother, I am not certain what to call certain foods. I do not say *ricotta*, because it sounds haughty to my ears, but I also cannot say *a'regautta*, either. Frankly, it just sounds silly. I avoid saying the word altogether. I just point and nod.

This bifurcation of the Italian language and Italian dialect also applies to Italian pastries and desserts.

Many dessert food names, like *gelato, panna cotta, biscotti, torrone, cannoli, cappuccino, tiramisù*, are said the same way in English as they are by Southern Italians in America. There are often mispronunciations of the proper Italian words, but Italian Americans and non-Italians pronounce them the same way. For example, Italian Americans and non-Italian Americans pronounce mascarpone as *mas-car-pohn* when they should say *mass-car-po-nay*, but that is niggling the details.

However, when we venture across Italy, pastries and desserts may have different names and are sometimes pronounced differently depending upon the region. As most of the Italians that immigrated to America are from the south, Southern Italian pastry names have become part of the Italian American language.

My mother gives a recipe to my wife for *zeppole*. She also writes down *sfinge* next to *zeppole* and then I remember, years ago, hearing the word *sfinge. Zeppole*, or *sfinge*, is an Italian pastry consisting of a deep-fried dough ball. You plop a ball of dough in a vat of boiling oil, fry it until it solidifies and *voilà*, you have a *zeppole*.

"They're easy to make," says my mother when I call her to talk about the recipe. "The oil ruins your pots, though," she adds.

"What do you call it?"

"What, are you writing a book?" she asks. "I call it *zeppole* and sometimes *sfinge*. We say both."

You can make *zeppole* either with a light and fluffy consistency, or with a more bread-like texture. Of course, a *zeppole* is not complete until you sprinkle it with powdered confectioners' sugar. Like many people in New York City, I eat *zeppole* at feasts like San Gennaro, but since my mother makes them, I have them at home, too.

Speaking of the San Gennaro festival, I have to talk about my *sfogliatella* experience. *Sfogliatella* means "small, thin leaf/layer," as the pastry's texture resembles stacked leaves. *Sfogliatella*, sometimes called lobster tail in English, is a shell-shaped filled Italian pastry native to Campania. In Neapolitan cuisine, there are two kinds of s*fogliatella*: *sfogliatella riccia* ("curly"), the "normal" version, and *sfogliatella frolla*, a less labor-intensive pastry that uses a short crust dough and does not form the *sfogliatella's* characteristic layers.

At fourteen years old, I am working as a busboy during the San Gennaro festival at Ferrara Bakery & Cafe in Little Italy, working to save money to take guitar lessons. I am amazed watching the bakers make *sfogliatella*. The dough is stretched out on a large table, then brushed with fat (butter, lard, shortening, margarine, or a mixture), then rolled into a log. Disks are cut from the end and shaped to form pockets. Then the inside is filled with custard using a snout shaped canvas apparatus. Since I can eat a pastry for free at Ferrara's, I have a *sfogliatella* with a cappuccino in the morning before I start my shift. The sun shaded by the Campari umbrella overhead, I savor each bite of my *sfogliatella*, feeling like I am king of the world. What other fourteen-year-old has this luxury?

Many years later, living above Court Street Pastry in Brooklyn, I wake up to the aromas of cheesecakes and almond-scented spices wafting in from the store below. By the time I get out of bed, the bakers have worked almost a full day. Court Street Pastry's crowning glory is the *sfogliatella*, or as they call it, the lobster tail. Their version of the lobster tail has a croissant-like exterior, though crunchier and more layered. The inside is filled with a mixture of whipped cream and custard, which must include nearly a pound of sugar. I buy a lobster tail every now and then and nibble on it first thing in the morning. It is so rich I cannot imagine anyone being able to eat a lobster tail in one sitting.

Then there is *struffoli*. *Struffoli* are puffy jelly-bean sized balls of fried dough which are crispy on the outside, light and airy on the inside. After making the honey balls, they are then drenched in citrus-scented warm honey and decorated with sprinkles.

According to folklore, *struffoli* bring good luck since their spherical shape is a symbol of abundance. In Sicily, *struffoli* are referred to as *pignolata*. In Abruzzo, they are called *cicerchiata*. They are mostly associated with Christmastime.

"I don't make *struffoli* anymore," says my mother. "Too much work."

Nowadays I get *struffoli* at Italian Bakeries to bring to my family on Christmas. I eat a few of them, but mostly I get them for everyone else. The truth is, for me, like so many people, *struffoli* remind me of the dessert table during the holidays. I love the way they pile up on a plate, even if a little haphazardly. I always eat the *struffoli* balls at the bottom of the mound—that is where all the honey accumulates. They are often decorated with candied red and green cherries, stripes of candied orange or lemon peel, candied nuts, candy, and edible ribbons. At the bakeries, I love how they are wrapped in a colorfully tinted cellophane. *Struffoli* look like Christmas.

No one corrects my pronunciation of *struffoli* or *zeppole*, *sfinge* or *sfogliatella*. They are Italian American words. They have not been hijacked by Americans who think they know better. These Italian pastries remain, not only as special words that only we possess, like secret pagan incantations that evoke the holidays, a piece of *italianità*, but also as superbly delicious desserts that are part of our unique cultural heritage.

I make sure to bring *struffoli* and other Italian pastries to my family on holidays. Everyone enjoys them. The mingling of the words, along with the delicious tastes, decorative colors, recalls the spirit of my grandparents. Reaching out to take a *struffoli*, I am stretching across place and time. I close my eyes, sink my teeth into the sweet soft texture. With each bite, I relive the words and phrases of a time gone by.

3

Sleeping with Fishes

When I am a teenager, my father makes *Linguine Vongole* before my mother gets home from work. While he makes dinner, my brother and sisters are setting the table. I'm in charge of tossing the salad. Just home from work himself, my father puts dinner together quickly. First, he slices garlic, sautés it in olive oil, then pours a can of Il Progresso white clam sauce in the pot.

"It's easier to make from the can," my father says. "And you don't have to clean the clams, which isn't an easy task."

Making fun of the name of the dish, I call it *Linguine Vaffanculo*, or linguine go fuck yourself in English.

What's interesting about my father's (and mother's) recipe for *Linguine Vongole* is that it's simple, easy to make and very delicious. You boil water, sauté the white (or red) clam sauce in olive oil and *presto* it's ready. It never occurs to me that we're eating food that comes from a can. And why would it? My parents are working people; they don't have time to prepare elaborate meals during the work week, although sometimes they still do.

Only later do I realize that our family eats in the tradition of Southern Italian cooking. That is, food made quickly with what's available on hand. There isn't a lot of fuss about how fresh the clams are.

Then for holidays, my mother makes canned *scungilli*, adding garlic sautéed in olive oil. Although *scungilli* can be amazingly simple to put together, it is extremely tasty. The pale, white flesh has a texture like *calamari*. Some serve it simply in a salad with garlic, sliced onion, red pepper flakes, lemon, oil, and vinegar. The dark outer layer, removed mostly for aesthetic purposes, is a great addition to a simple pasta with marinara sauce. Whether served chilled in an *insalata di mare* or hot in a marinara sauce, *scungilli* is a staple of Italian American cuisine.

"Your father liked it with oil and vinegar; my brother, your uncle, liked it with spicy marinara sauce. So, I made it both ways."

"How do you like it?" I ask.

"I never ate it. I hated it."

The word *scungilli* is the Neapolitan dialect word for conch, which in standard Italian is *conchiglia. Scungilli* has a pleasant briny flavor and a dense, meaty texture. For Americans from Southern Italy, it is perhaps reminiscent of a time when their ancestors lived near the ocean. Today, it can be hard to find fresh conch; it's mostly found in Italian markets, stores like D. Coluccio & Sons, partially cooked and frozen or in cans. My mother insists on buying the Lamonica brand.

"You can have it in your closet for a hundred years," my mother says. "When you open it, the conch will be fresh like you just caught it that day."

And it's true. I pick up a can of Lamonica *scungilli* and then eat it many months later. I can't believe how fresh it tastes.

"What's funny," my mother adds, "is that when you get *scungilli* fresh from the market, it can be rough. Lamonica's is always tender."

"Why is that?" I ask.

"How do I know?" she barks. "Maybe cooking it makes it tender," she adds, gently.

Although not as popular today as *calamari*, or even octopus and eel, *scungilli* is one of the dishes Italian Americans prepare for a holiday spread, especially for the Feast of the Seven Fishes on Christmas Eve.

Ironically, Crazy Joe Gallo is between plates of *scungilli* at Umberto's Clam House when gunmen enter and open fire. Crazy Joe, wounded, makes it to the sidewalk and dies, leaving the world with one of the most iconic photos of a murdered Mafia boss.

"What other seafood dishes did you make?" I ask my mother.

"I made a cold seafood salad."

"How do you make it?"

"*Scungilli*, scallops, shrimp, crab meat and sometimes octopus."

"Why sometimes octopus?"

"First of all, I couldn't always get it. Secondly, do you know how they prepare octopus?"

I shake my head no.

"They pound it on rocks to tenderize it. I saw that when I was a kid at the Fulton Fish Market; that image never left me."

"That sounds horrible."

"You're telling me?"

"What do you put in a seafood salad?"

"After you prepare the seafood, you add diced garlic, lemon and vinegar."

"That's all?"

"Are you kidding me? It costs fifty dollars, more if you add the octopus."

"How many people does it serve for fifty dollars?"

"Six people. And it's not even a meal; it's an appetizer."

Years later, my father is in his last stages of pancreatic cancer. We bring him home from the hospital.

"Just make him comfortable," the doctor says.

"What would you like to eat?" we ask my father. He is weak and pale, hardly able to keep his eyes open.

He feebly asks for Linguine with White Clam Sauce, *Linguine Vongole*.

We order the food. No time or energy to make it.

Now we are at the table, my mother, father, brother and two sisters, eating.

My father twirls the linguine on his fork and attempts to lift it to his mouth. He can't.

"Help Dad," shouts my brother Frank at me. I'm closer to my father.

"Can I help you?" I plead.

"No, I can't eat," my father says.

And although he doesn't eat the *Linguine Vongole,* it's the last food he'll ever taste.

4

Letter from Naples

Located in the middle of Grand Street, just one store down from
Ferrara Bakery & Cafe, E. Rossi & Company opened in 1910. It is one of
the last remaining authentic stores in Little Italy.

"Initially," says Ernie Rossi, grandson of the owner, "we sold news-
papers and magazines. Then we began publishing translation books, en-
abling native Neapolitans to translate their dialect into standard Italian
and also into English. E. Rossi & Company even provided services to
help people write postcards to home. This then led to the publishing and
selling of sheet music, mainly of Neapolitan songs." Word got around;
the store soon became a global center for publishing Neapolitan music.
They received compositions, in the style of the *Canzone Napoletana* tradition, from South America, the United States and Europe.

"I often say that you could trace the footsteps of the Neapolitan
song tradition in the store's archives," adds Ernie.

Many who walk by the store do not know its history. Looking at
the store from the outside, it's easy to see why.

The store window is stacked with religious statues, images of
saints, and parking signs. One warns: "You Taka My Space, I Breaka
You Face." Inside the store are more statues and signs, piles of kitch-
en supplies, Neapolitan espresso makers, molds for cannoli shells, pasta
cutters, T-shirts, and other memorabilia. Despite the apparent chaos,
Ernie can find anything at a moment's notice.

"What are your early memories of the store, Ernie?" I ask.

"Well, I was born and raised in the shop," Ernie says. "I would come in to dust the items on the shelves, the saints, the Italian horns, kitchen appliances, earning a dollar a week. After a while, I asked my uncle to give me a raise to one dollar and twenty-five cents."

"Did he give it to you?"

"Eventually, yes." He laughs.

"Do you remember how the publishing business started?" I ask.

"One of the first songs that my grandfather published was 'A Cartulina 'e Napule [Postcard from Naples]." It was sung by Gilda Mignonette, but written in New York City by Pasquale Buongiovanni and Giuseppe De Luca in 1927. The song is about a young Neapolitan, now living in America, who receives a postcard from his mother.

"The words are in Neapolitan dialect, not standard Italian. The lyrics were very meaningful to the newly arrived immigrants in this country, reminding them of their native country and the family they abandoned. The song was even successful in Naples, too."

"My father told me that he carried Gilda Mignonette's bags into the theater to sing," says Ernie. "One time she was roughed up by the Mafia when they tried to shake her down for payments on the success of 'A Cartulina 'e Napule."

"He told me that, even after being roughed up, when she got on stage, she made a hand gesture at the Mafia goons who were now in the audience."

"Another song that my grandfather published was Comm'è Bella 'a Stagione." It was written by Rodolfo Falvo and Gigi Pisano in 1924.

"Then, in the 1960s, Connie Francis did an album of Italian songs. Among those songs was Comm'è Bella 'a Stagione,' which became a big hit," Ernie adds.

The interesting thing, Ernie tells me, is that many of the Neapolitan songs then became American hits, when translated into English. Songs like O Solo Mio became It's Now or Never, a big hit song for Elvis. I Have But One Heart, originally O Marenariello, was recorded in 1947 by Vic Damone and became a big hit. It was even recorded by Sinatra.

"The songs have beautiful melodies. That's why they were picked up by American producers," says Ernie. "The songs have you laughing or crying. Sometimes both."

"My father told me that he was about to publish a song that Caruso was going to perform, but then Caruso suddenly died. Sadly, my father did not remember the name of the composition. Maybe when I go through the many cases of music, I'll find that song."

"That would be a great discovery," I say.

"I have a few rooms in storage where I've kept the sheet music. I wish that I were able to read and write music and had more time. I would love to go through the archive, one by one. It's going to take time and money. Between the high storage rent, and the pandemic, we have no revenue coming in. We were already finding it difficult to keep the business going before the pandemic, but the last few months have made it even harder to pay the bills. We're now reaching out to the public. I even have a GoFundMe page.

"I promised my dad I would keep his own father's name alive, by keeping the store open. I am hoping that PBS does a special on the history of the store. Maybe they'll turn the store into a museum someday."

Ernie dreams that someone famous will record one of his original songs and turn it into a hit. Ernie and I often play in the store together, sometimes accompanying each other or performing solo. We often regale the customers—many of whom are from all over the world. He often plays his favorite—*Far L'Amore Con Te* (Making Love With You)—which he wrote for his wife, Margaret. Years ago, Ernie and I played for Rosetta Papiro and her daughter, visiting from England, who stumbled upon the store on their New York City trip. Rosetta is now a dear Facebook friend; we stay in touch.

"Maybe someone famous will turn one of my songs into a hit and I could stay open for a few more years," he says. "Any entertainer that comes in, I play the song for them." This has included Dion and John Sebastian. He's even performed the song for director Francis Ford Coppola.

"Did you ever play the song for Jimmy Roselli?" I ask, knowing that Roselli, a contemporary of Sinatra, frequented the store and even sold his own albums there.

"He used to come in for one thing," Ernie says, chuckling, "to buy big, heavy frying pans to make his steaks and veal cutlets."

5

Daiquiris in Havana

Since my mother's fallen a few times, breaking her hip for the second time now, my brother Frank and I spend more time together at the hospital, at the rehab. We used to be close, going out together, working together. To pay for college, we even worked as hotel doormen during a strike, clutching on to each other for dear life.

Now we take walks to get coffee while making visits to the rehab. We talk about working out, staying in shape, work. I do not tell him, but I still consider him my best friend. So much history. Too much between us. Too much that only we have shared. My sisters did not share our experience. Coming from the projects, going to elite schools—and then trying to rationalize the disconnect between those two worlds. Which left us both feeling confused and empty. The world of the projects doesn't understand the world of an elite private college and the people that attended it. The world of the elite private college and the life that issues from it, cannot grasp the world of the projects.

"How's work?" Frank asks. His questions are now often an attempt to dodge speaking.

"Things are fine," I say tersely. I am brief because I feel that he doesn't really care about my response. Yes, he cares about me. He loves me. He's always been by my side and I believe always will be. Despite the distance between us now.

"How's your work?" I ask him, trying to throw the dodge at him.

"Good. Tough. Stock market is all over the place."

"Making money?"

"The worse it does, the better I do," he says.

He's not hiding anything in his dodge. I just think Frank doesn't want to talk about stuff. As a kid, he was the talker and I was the silent one. Now our situations have reversed. I'm over-talkative and Frank hardly says anything. Not just to me. To everyone. He'll call one of my sisters, mumble a few questions and then not say anything.

My mother's falls give him a reason to talk, however. He can talk about things, about how she is doing, the plans for her future. About what I need to do. All this, without talking about himself. In fact, he's annoyed often about the whole situation.

"You coming to see Mom tomorrow?"

"I'm going to try to come mid-day, work the rest of the day at the rehab," I say.

The next day he calls me at 7 a.m. Which is annoying.

"You going to Mom?"

"Yes, I'm going to Mom, like I said yesterday."

"OK, just checking."

It's his way of dealing with his anxiety.

"Yeah, it's your way of harassing me," I say.

And he asks "What?" like he doesn't understand what I'm saying. Of course he understands. He's just going to poke and poke to get what he wants.

And despite this back and forth, there's no anger. We're both anxious. My sisters as well. And all the grandchildren. Everyone's nervous because my mother is her own worst enemy. Even after falling a few times, breaking a hip, a vertebra, she still drinks wine at night, still self-medicates with Xanax and firmly believes none of this affects her steadiness.

"We should spend more time together," I tell Frank. "Why haven't we done this after all these years?" As I say this I'm thinking of the Havana scene in The Godfather where Michael and Fredo have a daiquiri together.

"How do you say daiquiri in Spanish?" asks Fredo.

"Daiquiri," says Michael.

As I talk to my brother, I'm thinking about that scene and who each would be. Am I Fredo? Or Michael? Or Sonny? Who would my father think I am? This is what's going through my mind as my mother's fate hangs by a thread.

6

Keeping it Sweet on Court Street

A few weeks ago, I went to shop at Caputo's Bakery Shop and Court Street Pastry, in my old neighborhood of Carroll Gardens. In these hard times, there is nothing like *ciabatta* bread and sweet, delicious pastries to bite back on that locked-in feeling. Thankfully, bakeries are considered essential businesses.

Stopping in at Caputo's first, I recognized a neighbor, Lorraine, who had lived across the street from me when I lived above Court Street Pastry. These days you can't tell who's who with everyone wearing masks. After I noticed her distinct bright red hair and then heard her strong Brooklyn accent, I shouted hello.

"What brings you back here, stranger?" she asked.

"Do you know what's it's like to go without *ciabatta* for a year?" I asked, rolling my eyes.

"This place draws you back."

We exchanged updates on our families. I told her about how my older son, who was half my height then, is now six foot four.

"The neighborhood looks so different," I said.

"It has changed a lot. Everything's more expensive," she added, rubbing her thumb and first two fingers together.

"The bakeries seem the same."

"They're still here," she said. "But the new neighbors aren't as big into these kinds of breads and pastries."

"When I lived here, people used to line up around the block on holidays to make their pilgrimage. They drove in from New Jersey, Staten Island, all over the New York area."

"Those were the days," she said.

"Do they still get the daily run of customers?"

"Well, many of the old-timers have moved out. The people here now don't buy in bag loads; they buy by the cookie, or by a single loaf of bread." Standing a good five feet tall, she waved her short arms from her round body as she spoke. A golden cross with the delicate body of Jesus nailed to it glittered from a chain around her neck.

When I lived above the Court Street Pastry shop, the neighborhood was dominated by bakeries. Every morning, I'd wake up to the aromas of cheesecakes and almond scented spices wafting in from the store below. By the time I got out of bed, the bakers had worked almost a full day. I was also smitten by the smell of fresh breads coming from Caputo's across the street. It was like my brain slept in a sugar paradise, flooded by tidal waves of cookies and breads smashing together in my dreams.

Being so close together, each bakery has a specialty. While Court Street Pastry makes pastries and confections, Caputo's specializes in breads and cookies. Baked on premises, Caputo's makes *ciabatta* and loaves stuffed with cheese or *prosciutto*. Fresh out of the oven, *ciabatta* is like eating doughy clouds. When you yank off chunks of the flat, long bread, it is fluffy and soft, practically melting in your mouth. You hardly chew it. The *prosciutto* bread is stuffed with wedges of *prosciutto* and baked with cheese.

Back then, I frequently saw the twin brothers who did most of the baking for Caputo's. They were short and stout, with curly light brown hair matting their strong, square faces. Built with thick forearms and stout legs, they looked Promethean. The twins frequently disappeared into the deep recesses of the bakery, perhaps even below the surface, nearer to the core of the earth, I imagined. Their faces red, I would see them emerge with trays of freshly baked breads on roller carts.

As if to not compete, Court Street Pastry doesn't make breads like Caputo's. They make sweets like *cannoli*, *sfogliatella*, cream puffs, and cookies, some smothered in chocolate, some dipped in colorful sprinkles. Court Street Pastry's crowning glory is the *sfogliatella*, or lobster tail, as it is also known, which has a croissant-like exterior, though crunchier and more layered. Filling the inside is a mixture of whipped cream and custard, which must include near a pound of sugar. They also make a Sicilian specialty called *mustazzola*. This confection is a flat brown cookie with lighter-colored dough molded in the form of the Baby Jesus lying on top. You only find *mustazzola* displayed on Easter and Christmas.

When I paid for bread at Caputo's, ready to head over to Court Street Pastry, Lorraine and I looked at each other through our masks.

"I would give you a hug, but you know," said Lorraine.

I nodded my head in agreement.

"It was great to see you. Say hi to the family."

It felt incredibly sad to just wave from six feet away.

As I left the store, I thought about the uniqueness of these bakeries. They come from a time and an era in New York City that has passed. Carroll Gardens is no longer a neighborhood of Southern Italians. Many who bought brownstones for, I don't know, fifteen to twenty thousand in the 1950s, sold them for one or two million dollars almost a decade ago. When I lived there, I remember often seeing refuse dumpsters parked outside of brownstones. The people who bought the brownstones refurbished the interiors, discarding '50s-era mirrors, aluminum ceilings and linoleum floors into garbage bins on the street. With their arrival, the neighborhood changed completely. The family-owned retail vacuum store disappeared. The garment store, where locals shopped to purchase fabric and sewing materials, was gone too. They were, perhaps, too common for the population moving in. And the little specialty shops, like the Salumerias and Italian food stores, closed as well. The people who moved in didn't buy that kind of food, at least in the same amounts.

The truth of the matter is that I often felt caught between these two worlds. I grew up in Long Island City, Queens. While it was not an Italian American neighborhood, it was blue-collar like Carroll Gardens. The stores in my neighborhood were hardware shops, shoemakers, and video rental places. There were no French bistros. When I left Queens, it was an insular place. Most of my friends did not go to college, or travel to Europe in summer. I escaped to experience the bigger world "out there," first living in California, then in Manhattan. Then, when I moved to Brooklyn, mainly out of circumstance, the boroughs were fast changing. I became part of that change. I become one of the colonizers. One of the occupiers.

I have one memory from a few years ago that says it all. Standing on line at Caputo's, an old lady, maybe five feet tall, shouted her order over the counter. "I'll take three *ciabattas*, three *prosciutto* breads, four pounds of cookies, in two boxes." I wondered how she'd carry it home. Then a young woman, next in line, made her request. "Can I just get a few of these in a bag," she said, pointing at chocolate-smothered cookies covered with sprinkles.

7

D. Coluccio & Sons

There are a few genuine Italian specialty food stores left in New York City. One of them is D. Coluccio & Sons. In what used to be the center of Little Italy in Brooklyn, D. Coluccio & Sons is sandwiched between Borough Park, Bensonhurst and Bay Ridge. Founded by Domenico Coluccio in 1962, D. Coluccio & Sons has the finest variety of imported Italian pastas, cheeses, baking products, prosciuttos, soppressatas, and delicious cakes available today in the tri-state area. Did I mention that they also make mozzarella on premises? You will often find the mozzarella still warm on their deli countertop display.

Immigrating from Marina di Gioiosa, a small town in southeastern Calabria, Italy, Domenico began importing foods that you could only get from his part of Calabria. This tradition of maintaining an inventory of unique food imports has continued today with his children: Luigi, Rocco, and Cathy.

I drove to the store in late April to shop and to see how things are going in the wake of the Coronavirus.

I had to queue out in front, along with other people, as the store now only allows five customers in at a time. Everyone must wear a mask and a pair of gloves (they provide the gloves) to enter. When it was my turn, I rushed into the store like a thief, grabbing a few essential items: a box of fresh pasta, packages of stuffed raviolis, olive oil, bottled artichokes, and a few bags of peperoncino flavored taralucci (a snack which is like a cross between a cracker and a pretzel). Of course, no visit to D. Coluccio & Sons is complete without at least one (or two) spicy soppressata(s). There is nothing like biting into a Coluccio soppressata. It is not a packaged food. Made with peperoncino and other flavors specific to Calabria, I always close my eyes and sigh when I take the first bite. Before the virus, when my wife and I had company, I would proudly serve sliced Coluccio Soppressata, stacked up next to Coluccio's Asiago cheese, and watch people's reactions after their first taste. Most would shake their heads and point at the delectable treat in disbelief.

Here is a little secret. I often wake up in the morning and cut a few pieces of Coluccio soppressata to eat first thing in the morning. When I roll out of bed. Before vitamins. Before anything. I eat as much soppressata as I want in the morning because I know I'll burn it off during the day.

As I was curious to learn more about how else the virus has affected the store, I called a few days later to see if I could talk to someone.

When I said I was calling from the *Red Hook Star Revue*, I was passed to Cathy, the founder's daughter.

I told her that I have long been a big fan of D. Coluccio & Sons and would love to chat about the impact of the Coronavirus.

Cathy was immediately friendly and warm.

"Importing is definitely slower," said Cathy. "But our inventory is completely stocked."

"I noticed all of the regular items are on the shelves," I said.

"We've done our best to adapt," Cathy added. "And because of our connections in Italy, we made adjustments to our business early on. In fact, we were among the first stores in New York City to require wearing masks and gloves and to limit the amount of people in the store at the same time."

"Has the virus changed the things people purchase?" I asked.

"People are buying more things to cook at home. Our pastas fly off the shelves. Our all-purpose double zero flour (also called *doppio zero*) has been immensely popular. People are doing a lot of baking at home:

breads, pastas and pizza. We also have fresh yeast and dry yeast, both of which have been in short supply everywhere."

"How has the community reacted to D. Coluccio & Sons staying open?" I asked.

"Everyone has been incredibly supportive," said Cathy. "One of the really wonderful things is the stories we hear. People making cakes and baking breads for each other, leaving them at the door. Neighbors, friends, and family. It's really sweet."

"When do you think you'll get back to normal?" I asked.

"Hopefully soon. This is not just another store. This is our family tradition. It goes back generations. In the meantime, we will continue bringing great food into people's homes in the safest way we can."

8

Taking the Cannoli

I can draw a dotted line from my childhood to the present with *cannoli* memories.

My father often took me to Little Italy before I was fourteen. He was immensely proud of his Italian heritage. Our pilgrimage followed nearly the same path of stores every time.

"You don't know what great music is," said my father when we visited E. Rossi & Company. As I scanned the aisles loaded with Italian knickknacks, like saints' statues, horse and carriage figures, and Neapolitan coffee machines, my father would point to the air, trying to make me listen to Jimmy Roselli's *Malafemmena* blasting from the speakers. Of course, I rolled my eyes.

Now at Umberto's Clam House we ate *scungilli* and *calamari*. He knew the waiters, made small talk with them.

"This is where Crazy Joe Gallo was shot out in the open," he whispered. I remembered the pictures from the papers of Crazy Joe splayed out on the ground, blood pouring from his head.

Having grown up in Little Italy, my father knew Mafia characters. He never wanted to be a mobster, but he was fascinated by their larger-than-life personalities and their lawlessness. To him, mobsters were like New York City cowboys.

Afterwards, we stopped by Café Roma to have a black coffee, share a *cannolo*, and then brought some home for the family. The *cannoli* were creamy, white and sweet.

Then, at fourteen, all grown up, I worked afternoons and nights at Ferrara Bakery & Café as a busboy during the San Gennaro Festival. My friend John's cousin, Emilio, was a pastry chef at that time; he got us the jobs, no questions asked about our age. I arrived in the afternoon before my shift. Having my permitted cappuccino and *cannolo*, I sat shaded under a Campari umbrella in the hot summer sun, looking like a king. During one late-night shift I made out with a girl my age who worked at Ferrara's. We found a hidden alcove in the basement where the ovens cooked the endless trays of pastries. With the sweet aromas swirling around us, we gave each other full-mouth kisses and rubbed our bodies together, like matches trying to light a fire.

The last night of the feast, John and I each took a hit of mescaline. I bussed tables, giggling the whole time, trying not to drop food trays on customers. I couldn't even look at John without falling over hysterically laughing. The green, red and white lights that hung from the lampposts were like glittering stars. They shone even brighter from the tears of laughter that filled my eyes. I can't imagine how insane we looked to the rest of the world.

So many Christmases, Easters. And the occasional cannolo here and there. I never ate a *cannolo* that wasn't from an Italian bakery. Why would I? In New York City, if you know where to go, you can devour a scrumptious *cannolo* anytime.

Only recently, at fifty-four, after all these years, I sought to learn more about *cannoli* history. I searched the internet. Were there any books on the subject? Not really, except for *cannoli* recipe books, some of which were self-published by someone's aunt or grandmother.

Then I came across Allison Scola, founder of Experience Sicily and The Cannoli Crawl. I wrote to Allison via Facebook Messenger, asking if she could point me to a book or other resource where I could learn more about *cannoli* history. Since we had many friends in common from our mutual interests in Italian American culture and studies, I thought that she might not think I was a random crazy person and would perhaps write back.

Lo and behold, a few days later, Allison messaged me back on Facebook. She sent me information that she had written about *cannoli* history. Allison comes from a lineage of *cannoli* makers, extending back to Sicily. She was initiated into the *cannoli* mysteries by her second cousin Pietro Buttitta, a retired, Palermo-trained pastry chef who founded and owned a *pasticceria* in Rome for over thirty years. Beginning his apprenticeship at fourteen, Pietro in turn learned the "secrets" of *cannoli*-making from his uncle Domenico Cuffaro in Bagheria, Sicily. Domenico's famous Bagherese establishment, Bar Aurora, was a social hub for adults and teenagers after World War II. It was called *Il salotto di Bagheria* (The Salon of Bagheria).

Allison generously sent me links to her writings and documents as well. Her generosity blew me away. The fact is everything I now know about *cannoli* can be attributed to Allison. I call her *Il Professore dei Cannoli*.

Allison and I spoke on the phone and had a Teams call and we finally met at the Piccolo Cucina at 75 Thompson Street in Soho, New York City. In addition to serving Sicilian-inspired cuisine, Piccolo Cucina makes *cannoli* in the Sicilian tradition; that is, with sheep's milk. As sheep's milk is not something easily found in the United States, some restaurants, like Piccolo Cucina, overnight it frozen from Italy.

When Allison arrived, wearing a facemask, I wasn't sure if it was her. I wasn't expecting her to be so tall; perhaps she wasn't expecting me to be so short. As soon as she took off her mask, I recognized her face from our online meetings. Allison is a very pretty woman.

We had a COVID embrace and sat down. Since Piccolo Cucina is one of the stops on her Cannoli Crawl, everyone at the restaurant knew her. She spoke in perfect Italian.

"Did you grow up speaking Italian?"

"No," she said, "I studied Spanish from middle school through college. Then I learned Italian when I started going to Italy, after college."

Having travelled extensively to Italy and learning the language, making connections with family, she has become a fount of knowledge on all things Italian. Allison explained that her business was greatly impacted by COVID. There are no tours to Sicily currently and giving Cannoli Crawls has not been an option. Her greatest passions have been put on hold for now. Things are slowly opening, however.

We then got down to business.

"Italians eat *cannoli* made from sheep's milk ricotta as opposed to cow's milk ricotta," she said.

"Are Italian *cannoli* less sweet?"

"It depends on where you're eating the *cannoli*. In cities like Palermo, they make the *ricotta* extremely sweet, with additives, so it lasts longer. If you're close to a sheep farm, you get your *ricotta* the next day. You don't need to add sugar to it. The *ricotta* has a delightful flavor, and the ricotta is lighter."

Allison continued.

"The tradition of making *cannoli* goes back to ancient Rome. And of course, making *cannoli* is inextricably tied to the seasons," said Allison, her blue eyes sparkling as we spoke.

"In Sicily, the wheat fields are harvested and then burn from the sun all summer long. In November, the grass starts to grow again, and the region's Mediterranean clover and grass fields turn green. In November, Sicily's clover fields look a lot like Ireland's fields of green.

"When the grass starts to green, it also gets sweet. The farmers keep the male and female sheep away from each other all summer, only letting them mate when the grass gets green and sweet. Sweet grass means sweet milk. As the sheep begin to mate, the female sheep begin to lactate. From November to May, with the rains washing over the farmlands, the grass has reached its peak sweetness. If timed right, sheep mate in October/November and give birth in February/March.

"*Ricotta* is a byproduct of cheese-making. To make cheese, you add rennet to sheep's milk and boil it, and it curds—that's the cheese. Rennet is acid from a lamb's stomach, a lamb that has never had anything other than its mother's milk. The liquid that doesn't curd is whey. You collect the whey separately from the curd, add more salt, and boil it again. That forms another round of curds that we call *ricotta*." The word *ricotta* means recooked in Italian. In other words, recooked whey.

According to folklore, Romans discovered whey when making cheese. Whey, the yellow liquid byproduct of cheese, was drained as garbage into the aqueducts. As it moved along the stone troughs, it curdled. Apparently, some genius, or perhaps someone who was really hungry, must have dipped a finger into the aqueduct to taste it. And, in so doing, history was made. It was like a "you put your chocolate in my peanut butter" moment.

The ancient Romans loved feasts and festivals. Two famous ones they celebrated, related to the harvest and growing season, were Carnevale and Saturnalia. Romans got kinky during Carnevale. They called it topsy-turvy. Some masters would switch roles with their servants. Some people would wear masks and pursue flings incognito. Sex in alleyways with people who didn't know each other. Anything could happen. It was like a wild open sex party. And nothing amps up an orgy like a *cannolo*.

Allison explained that the Romans placed the *ricotta* cheese in a typical griddle cake and rolled it up like a tortilla—a tube. It was kind of the equivalent of an ice-cream cone that the ancients ate while walking down the street.

"It's intentionally shaped like a penis," said Allison, making me blush a little bit.

"I have been immature most of my life," I said, "and I've associated many things with a penis, but never *cannoli*."

"The Romans were very openly sexual. And they celebrated sexuality in a way that we don't today. People wore penis pendants. There were penis symbols on doors, representing fertility, good luck and power."

This made me think of the poems of Catullus, which would quiet a roomful of intellectuals even today.

Then the Arab harems of Sicily during the ninth and tenth centuries modernized this ancient recipe—also with the intention of it representing a penis. The ladies of the Emir's court created the *cannoli* closer to the ones we know today using sugar cane and candied fruit to put it over the top.

After a light lunch, it was time to have Sicilian *cannoli*. The *cannoli* were relatively small. Unlike the smooth white texture of American *cannoli,* like you'd get at Ferrara's, the ricotta *cream of the cannolo Siciliano* is slightly yellowed and earthy. It tastes more like cheese.

I ate my *cannolo* in a few bites, as Allison and I talked. A tube filled with thick cream, I thought to myself. How did I never associate it with a penis? Then I remembered taking mescaline as a kid during my shift at Ferrara's, making out with girls in the catacombs of Ferrara's. I didn't realize it then, but John and I were marking our version of topsy-turvy. We were licking off the sweet cream of lust that only youth can offer.

After Allison and I parted, I walked over to E. Rossi & Company, one store over from Ferrara's in Little Italy, to ask Ernie to play some Jimmy Roselli music. And, while I was there, I picked up some *cannoli* before I got on the train to go home.

9

You Know My Father?

My sister Camille and I are visiting my father in the hospital. It is now month two of my father's three-month pancreatic cancer prognosis.

He's paler now than he was even just a week ago. The morphine makes him look groggy and dazed.

"How are you, Dad?" I ask. I don't really understand what he's going through. I don't have any sense of the pain he is in. The despair he feels. Though no excuse, I haven't seen many people sick like my father before. Our family didn't grow up surrounded by disease. We had other problems.

"I'm great," my father replies sarcastically. "Did you bring my cigarettes?" He sounds slurred and jerky from the opiate.

"No cigarettes, just whiskey," I answer.

Then, pointing to my sister Camille I say, "Nurse, can we move this bed into another room?"

"What?" says Camille.

"You know my father," I say. "People are coming to kill him." I'm mimicking the scene in *The Godfather* when Virgil Sollozzo's men come to kill Vito Corleone in the hospital.

Now my sister gets the joke and makes a frown face.

"Stupid," she says.

"Dad, we're going to move you to a different room."

This would usually make my father laugh. But not now, not this time.

"I can't joke right now," my father says.

My father's eyes are watery and bulbous. Suddenly, I see him very differently. He is hanging by a thread. I can't detect his usual joking nature. And the fact is, there's nothing funny about what's going on. A rush of realization comes to me. My father is dying. He's dying fast and furiously, like a man falling into a deep dark pit. How much longer does he have? Will he die in a month like the doctors said?

And now my idiotic joke just seems like an insensitive thing to do or say to my father. He's not cheered up. I'm not cheered up. I'm cold and empty like a zombie whose soul has just been ripped out by a devil.

Now my father is putting his hand up to his mouth, as if he's smoking a cigarette. My sister and I look at each other, slightly giggling. As fucked up as this is, it's funny that he's hallucinating.

Our nervous laugh turns to silence now. My father's urge to smoke is powerful, so deep in his unconsciousness, that he's dreaming of smoking even in his lurch towards death.

I laugh a little again, but it's more like a chill has swept up my spine. I shake off the jitters, as Camille and I each stroke one of my father's arms, standing on either side of his bed.

10

The Pizza Histories

Brother Cresci stuck the knife deep into Brother Silvestro's neck, killing him in one stroke. He had completed his task—to ensure that *The Secret Order of Pizza Napuletana* maintain its strict code of silence. The year was 1650.

On one of his insomniac walks through the monastery, Brother Silvestro Bruni had discovered documents exposing the history of *The Secret Order of Pizza Napuletana*. His fate may have been different if he hadn't then written letters to a cousin in Rome, revealing details of the *The Secret Order of Pizza Napuletana*. The documents Brother Silvestro found told of the Pythagorean origins of the sect, explaining the exact dimensions of the pizza circles. They also offered, in detail, the symbolism of the triangular slice, its reference to the Father, Son, and the Holy Ghost. The writings were in Coptic, Greek, Hebrew and Latin.

Brother Cresci was merely protecting the sanctity of the order. Among the trove that Brother Silvestro had uncovered were manuscripts expounding on the ancient Hermetic origins of the sect, its beginnings in Ancient Egypt, migration to the Middle East, and then to Europe. But most importantly, there was a section relating the story of the Last Supper—the version which was suppressed for centuries and which could not be told. It went something like this:

"My brothers, tonight one of you will betray me," Jesus said. "Despite this, I love you all," he added trying to hide his feeling of disappointment. "In fact, tonight, I still want to order out for pizza. I love you, my brothers, and despite one bad egg, we will enjoy this night like other nights before it."

They all insisted that they were loyal to him. Murmurs of "What do you mean, Lord?" and "How could you say this, Lord?" were heard. They were dumbfounded and hurt.

Jesus bowed his head and, gathering all his strength, he lifted his face again to look at the disciples—his dark brown eyes watery and swollen.

"OK, who wants what?" he asked.

"Lord, I would like mushrooms on my pizza," John said with a big smile on his face; he knew Jesus liked mushrooms, too. He was always happy for Jesus. Like a little brother, John followed Jesus everywhere, copying his every move.

"Extra cheese, please," said Mark, the gloomy one. He looked rakish with his shaggy beard and dirty clothes. Though they were all unshaven and dirty, Mark was the worst. He stunk even worse than Lazarus after being dead for three days. It is said that Jesus had to hold his mouth to keep from vomiting on the stench of Lazarus's resurrected carcass.

"What kind of meat can I have on mine, my Lord?" Judas asked. The others eyed each other and became silent upon hearing his question.

* * *

More than a thousand years later, the true origin of the Holy Pizza was still maintained in the strictest secrecy. *The Secret Order of Pizza Napuletana* had become one of the largest underground militias—equaling the Knights Templars and the Teutonic Knights. Its secrets were well kept for many hundreds of years. But there was always gossip abounding. Even the kings and queens were denied access to the order's secrets.

For instance, in 1775, King Ferdinand I, determined to penetrate the inner sanctum of the order's mysteries, disguised himself as a commoner and visited a poor neighborhood in Naples. Although he publicly declared that he merely wanted to sink his teeth into the local Neapolitan pizza, the order was suspicious of his intentions. The next day one of King Ferdinand's spies was found wearing women's clothing rifling through documents in a secret vault.

For his transgression, the spy was drowned in a cauldron of scalding tomato sauce. Some say he was knowingly eaten by the secret order in an act of brutal retaliation.

The order continued to operate in utter silence, protecting its confidentiality, performing whatever violence was required. It was out of step with the times. Even the Catholic Church had undergone reforms; Latin was no longer required at every Mass and even the poor weren't required to relinquish their gold teeth to add to the church's coffers.

Finally, in 1885, *The Secret Order of Pizza Napuletana* underwent radical changes.

"We've had too many close calls," shouted Cardinal Di Figlio, high priest of *The Secret Order of Pizza Napuletana* by night and a low Cardinal in the Catholic Church by day. He was surrounded by the knights who had sworn fealty to the order, staking their lives for the sake of maintaining its silence. During the meeting, a delivery of pies was brought in from the kitchen.

"I'm afraid we have to capitulate to the pressures that surround us," Di Figlio said wearily. He was severe, unyielding. Only a radical like Di Figlio could dare take on thousands of years of history in a single stroke.

"We have to share the recipes," he added.

All stopped eating.

Brother Frescobaldi dropped his pizza, his mouth wide open. Brother Ripetti nearly choked on his pepperoni slice.

"The Queen is coming to Naples in a few weeks. I propose that we make a special pizza for her," he said, waving his hands. "Maybe we can make this pizza resemble the colors of the Italian flag, tomato for red, mozzarella for white and basil for green."

The knights looked upon him dejectedly, as if he'd asked them to shout the hermetic secrets of the order to anyone and everyone.

"Finally, I suggest that we name this recipe after the Queen calling it the Pizza Margherita."

This last statement was received by a throng of sighs.

"Brothers, my goal is to save the true secrets of our order, the holy pizza prayers, the hermetic practices and the truth about the Last Supper. We will give them the ingredients, the recipes. They will think they have discovered the final truth, but it will just be delicious little morsels that we have thrown them."

The Secret Order of Pizza Napuletana underwent a haircut and a facelift. Its name was changed to *Associazione Vera Pizza Napoletana* (True Neapolitan Pizza) and its secret texts were hidden in the vaulted chambers of St. Peters. Only the Pope would possess the keys to the crypts where the sacred texts were stored. To confound the public, the *Association of the True Neapolitan Pizza* published copious books on the correct way to make pizza.

But the world would forever be on the wrong trail.

11

The History of Fear

My sister Gina calls me after she read my story.

"Oh my God, why did you write that stuff about Dad?" She's not frantic, but she's upset that I wrote publicly about our father's gambling problems.

"I write about our family because it's hard to write about," I say. "Because it matters."

"You know Mom can't see this story," she adds. And I know that too. Too many details about how he borrowed money, and the general despair we all felt. Though it was an almost daily discussion when we were kids, it's now a subject to be avoided. When my father died twenty-five years ago, he became saintly. His earthly sins were buried in his grave.

"I know. I don't want her to see it. I don't want to upset her."

"Well, I'm happy for you," Gina says. She means it, too. "I'm thrilled for your success."

My father's worst critic, when he was alive, was my mother. I remember how it upset me to hear her talk to him. Before she moved out of our house for a few weeks, her attacks on him became even more vitriolic.

"If you have to get another job, do it," she said. "I'm working all day, come home to make dinner, clean the house then sell jewelry at night," she added, raising her voice. Then. "I don't care if you never come home."

This last statement clanged off the project building walls and rang throughout the house, like a rusted metal bell hammered on a steel stairwell.

My father didn't respond. He had swallowed so much guilt, he couldn't speak. The guilt stuffed his mouth, froze his throat and sank into his stomach. From there it went straight into the infinite space of his soul. Enough guilt to fill the universe. He looked down at his crossword puzzle and tapped his foot in his slipper. In silence.

Hearing the shriek in my mother's voice bothered me as a kid. Why did she have to be so mean? Now I know better. She was out of her mind with worry. How will we pay rent? How will we make it to the next day?

She went on long into the night. Her voice searing and desperate.

But nowadays, my mother only praises my father. About how smart he was. How talented. How handsome. The truth is they did love each other very much. You could always see that. They hugged each other. Spoke kindly most of the time. And they enjoyed each other's company. It was the gambling that poisoned their relationship.

And so now I am the Fredo of the family. The snitch. I say things. I write things. You have to understand that this tradition of keeping your mouth shut is very old. It goes back centuries. It is the modern form of omertà, or code of silence. Omertà is a dialect form of the word umiltà, "humility," in reference to the code of submission of individuals to the group interest. Being taciturn, you're serving the needs of a greater good. Shut up, don't upset your mother. Keep your mouth closed, show respect.

The roots of our family silence extend back hundreds of years. It begins in Sicily and Southern Italy in general. Since Sicily was a crossroads for empires, it was often occupied by foreign powers. The Greeks, Romans, Moors, Normans, Bourbons, and Nazis, to name a few. Average Sicilians couldn't count on government, or society, to help them. This was only compounded when Garibaldi united Italy. Although Garibaldi recruited the South to fight the Bourbons in the North, he then abandoned the South. The South suffered from lack of infrastructure: schools, hospitals and so on. And the villages were under feudal rule; if you were a laborer, there was simply no way out. They were trapped, like mice in a cage. The only thing they could count on was family. Family was their refuge. When Vito Corleone says, "Never let anyone outside the family know what you're thinking," he's referring to the tradition of omertà.

Given the tumultuous nature of Sicily's history, its notable writers—Leonard Sciascia, Luigi Pirandello, Giuseppe di Lampedusa, Elio Vittorini, and Maria Messina—have described an overarching narrative of *paura storica*, or history of fear. Fear of the outsider. Fear of the unknown.

In writing about my family, I've committed a sin. I've broken a long-held tradition of silence. It's as if I've woken my father from the grave. Only I can see him looking at me disapprovingly. Behind curtains, behind doors. Walking the halls of our project apartment, alone. Like I unleashed fear of the outsider on our family.

And while my sister and other siblings might be slightly wounded by my breaking the silence, they are also happy for me. And proud of me. That's another contradiction in the Southern Italian soul. The love for family is so strong, you can hate someone, or really be annoyed at them, maybe never even talk to them, but still love them, still want the best for them. This isn't always true with every family, but it's true with mine.

So, I continue to tell our story, our history of fear.

12

Di Fara Pizza

I live down the block from Di Fara Pizza on J Street in Midwood, Brooklyn.

I must admit that I have a love-hate relationship with Di Fara.

Let's talk about the hate part first. Maybe hate is too strong a word. It's just that all of the fanfare around Di Fara annoys me.

Mostly when I pass Di Fara there's a long line wrapped around the block. And you can tell that the line is comprised of people from other neighborhoods. Midwood is mostly Orthodox Jewish and working class. And, at least for the moment, it is not a hipster neighborhood. You don't see a lot of nose rings, hair-buns and knitted summer hats. But on the Di Fara line, there's a sea of nose-rings and ironic facial hair. What's annoying about this is that there's always a line. It doesn't matter who's on it, but there's a line, which makes going to Di Fara like a Mission Impossible episode. Also, from my experience, seeing ironic facial hair is an indicator that my rent is about to go up. But that's another story.

If you must go to Di Fara and are willing to wait on the line, the whole situation becomes desperate once you're inside. People are milling about, jockeying to get up to the counter, waving cash at the counterperson, afraid their turn will be missed. It feels like waiting on line at the DMV.

Then, when it's your turn at the counter, you're lucky enough to spend $5 per slice. And the truth is, the pizza isn't always great. But it is often very good.

What bugs me is that the average slice of pizza in New York City used to be decent. But now getting a good slice of pizza is an event. You have to go to a brick-oven pizzeria to get good pizza, for the most part. Most pizza places use generic cheese, sauce, and dough. And they probably don't know how to perform the magic that makes those basic ingredients become something mouthwatering and delicious.

Domenico "Dom" De Marco, who opened Di Fara Pizza in 1965, knows how to make pizza. Born in the Province of Caserta in Italy, Dom knows his way around Italian food. Many of the ingredients are imported from Italy; their distinct flavors create a taste that can't be replicated. And Di Fara's retro oven transmutes these already fine ingredients into something altogether different. Until recently, each pizza pie was handcrafted by Dom. You would often see him cutting the basil and pouring the virgin olive oil directly on each pizza. With several of his children supporting him in the kitchen, Dom is less seen these days. There are locations now in both Midwood and Williamsburg, fully family owned and operated. And Dom's children will continue to make great pizza as long as people are willing to wrap around the block to buy it.

13

Louis Prima Jr.

Life has a funny way of coming full circle sometimes.

Someone I don't know writes me about a piece I had placed in the *Red Hook Star Review* on Louis Prima a few weeks prior. That someone, my new friend Charlie Diliberti, then tells me that Louis Prima's son, Louis Prima Jr., tours around the country playing New Orleans style jazz, like his father. In fact, he knows Louis Prima Jr., he says. Would I like to meet him? Charlie also tells me that he speaks Sicilian. Then we write back and forth about our Sicilian origins.

I'm going to pause here for a moment to connect the time travel elements of all of this. The piece that Charlie reads is inspired by my leaning backward in time to explore my dad's musical interests. He was a big fan of Louis Prima. And by writing the piece, it connects me to the future. To new friends.

A few weeks later, Charlie writes saying that Louis Prima Jr. and the Witnesses are playing at The Cutting Room in Manhattan. Would I like to meet him there? Of course, I say yes.

When I get to The Cutting Room, Charlie has filled three tables with friends and family. He introduces me and my twenty-three-year-old son, Thelonious, whom I drag along, to the people at the table. They are friendly, talking and having fun.

Like in Spinal Tap, when Prima Jr. and the Witnesses take the stage, their set starts at volume eleven. Not ten. Eleven. From the first note, they erupt on the stage, bucking and kicking, stomping and romping. Never missing a single note. They are smack on.

Meanwhile, the room is eager and wanting, but they haven't yet caught up to the high velocity of the band. They're still eating, having only had a few drinks. Prima Jr. is hopping around and singing, like his father. The band follows his antics, bouncing on one foot in unison, while playing their instruments with incredible accuracy.

And like his father, Prima Jr. has a lead sax player and a female vocalist. Marco Palos, lead sax player and arranger, also writes some of the songs. Kate Curran, like Prima Sr.'s vocalists, can hit the high notes and make it sound easy. And she too plays the on-stage theatrics. She's the steady to Prima Jr.'s wild gymnastic performance. She's shapely and exotic, hand on hip like Bettie Boop.

The band then plays a few songs written by Marco, Prima Jr. and A.D. Adams from their two albums *The Wildest* and *Blow*. The songs are reminiscent of Prima Sr.'s style, but they are new and fresh. Marco is impeccably dressed, tall and handsome. He is debonair expertly playing his sax, like it's a walk in the park. Meanwhile, the whole band is singing harmonies. And the whole band is stomping on one foot now, as if trying to tilt the stage. I imagine that even the street outside The Cutting Room is on a slant, parked cars rolling down the street. I hold on tight to my beer, so it won't slide off the table.

The sound level, now at twelve, threatens to blow the roof off the venue.

As Louis and the band bounce and hop around, the venue is hot and humid. It's a rainy and sticky night. Somehow there isn't enough air-conditioning flowing into the room. All the players are mopping their faces with rags. I'm sweating too and I'm not running laps like they are.

Four songs in, the audience is now warming up. The band's intoxicating energy is infectious.

The audience is no longer just passively watching. They are part of the show.

As I look around, most people in the audience are out of their seats, some are whipping napkins around over their heads. This is a party. *This ain't no foolin' around.*

I get up to go to the bathroom. When I come back, I'm grabbed by the hand and spun by a woman I don't know. Now I'm dancing, too.

Even my son Thelonious is bopping around in his seat. He winces at me dancing with a stranger, as if saying *Dad, how could you? You look ridiculous.*

After a break, the band comes back on, taking turns singing songs. They are all excellent singers.

I now notice that Prima Jr. has slipped behind the drum kit. Everybody plays every instrument in this band, it seems. They perform lively versions of songs like "Born on the Bayou" by Creedence and Elton John's "Saturday Night's Alright for Fighting" revealing their rock-music roots.

The crowd is now almost all out of their seats. It's pandemonium. Now fully lathered up, Prima Jr. returns to the mic, singing a few of Sr.'s old hits like "Just a Gigolo" and "Buona Sera"; the audience is now totally wild, singing along with every lyric, punching their fists with every stomp and stop. I see two guys in the audience fall to the ground while dancing drunkenly. This scene has become an orgiastic Mardi Gras.

After their last song, Prima Jr. comes off stage. He has basically just run a marathon. Still wearing a fancy Vegas performer suit, he walks toward me. I ask him if I can take a picture. Even though he's been running on stage for two hours, in the picture I take, he looks cool and relaxed. I, on the other hand, look haggard, like I've run into a Mack truck.

After the picture, I thank him with a hug. I think to myself that we're about the same age. Our parents would be about the same age. It's as if our fathers introduce us from the past. Wait, how could that be?

I leave The Cutting Room thinking about how things come full circle. How little gestures or events can change the future. How life can be so ironic. That I'm looking at a picture of me and Louis Prima Jr., which I wish I could show my dad—mainly because he's responsible for all of this.

Sometimes life just makes sense in some way that can't be explained.

14

Laugh Clown Laugh

My eighty-four-year-old mother had taken another bad fall. This time, however, Mom had broken her vertebrae and was rushed to the hospital. Two weeks later, she was still in intensive care, her oxygen levels frighteningly low, her vital systems ebbing, but now she had moments of clarity. The doctors said she may never walk again. My brother, my two sisters and I took turns going to the hospital, making sure she hardly had a moment alone.

"You're going to have to use oxygen from now on," said my brother Frank, knowing that my mother was girding for a fight. "And you can't smoke anymore, either" he added. It was expected that Frank's approach would be to directly stab, as opposed to luring Mom into making better decisions.

"Let me tell you something," my mother snarled, her dark eyes on fire, pointing her bony finger at Frank. "I'll purposely light up a cigarette with the oxygen contraption hooked up when you come to visit and blow us both up."

Camille, Lynn and I cracked up in nervous laughter. My mother, however, wasn't exactly laughing. At that moment, she might have tossed an explosive at Frank. Out of the love in his heart, if Frank could put my mom in amber to make her last a million years, he would. Even as my mother screamed "you sonofabitch" while he sealed her in the amber, he'd have a loving smile on his face, tears streaming down his cheeks. "We're all going to die, Mommy," he'd say, "but not you."

There were a few weeks where we wondered if she'd make it out of the hospital. The fall only exposed her already poor condition. We knew that her lungs, after sixty-five years of smoking, were practically lumps of coal. But we didn't know that because her lungs were so depleted her body was also oxygen deprived. She had needed an oxygen tank even before the fall. Despite this, my mother refused to have an oxygen tank at home, even though the doctors said she couldn't leave the hospital without one. And in order to be discharged from the hospital she had to get her oxygen up to a semi-normal level. Owing to her Herculean willpower, faithfully doing the therapy and exercises, she increased her breath and strength enough to be released from the hospital. And to our utter amazement she stopped smoking. This was no small miracle. Up until that point, she defended the right to smoke like it was written in the Declaration of Independence. Life, liberty and the pursuit of tobacco.

After she was released, it was as if we'd brought home a different person. Always self-sufficient and stubbornly independent, she was now reduced to using a walker and shackled to an oxygen tank. And being afflicted with a combination of degenerative osteoporosis and neuropathy that numbed the sensation in her hands and feet, she just couldn't count on her feet anymore.

Clearly, Mom needed a home attendant. She adamantly resisted the idea.

"I don't want a stranger in my house," she said, her face wrinkled with pain.

"You're going to need someone with you, and we can't be there all of the time," said Camille. My mother had developed a strangling dependency on Camille. Camille and her husband, Simon, lived in the same building complex. They took her to the doctors, shopped for her and did the million little things no one sees every day, all of the time. Yet Mom delivered her sharpest attacks on Camille and Simon, as if they were the cause of her medical issues and shrinking physical abilities.

"Don't tell me what I need," snapped my mother in response to Camille.

"We can't be there all of the time with you," said Frank, chiming in. "I'll pay for the attendant."

"I have the money," Mom shot back in a nasty tone. This wasn't the generous and kind mother we'd known all of our lives. Yes, she'd always been firm, demanding that you do what was necessary. "If you want to go to college, then you'll have to work," she said when we were younger. She could be hard and sharp, but never mean. This other person was mean.

We managed to convince her to have an attendant come to her house during the weekdays. But then there was the question of her being alone at night.

A few days later, Frank called me.

"We're going to have to take turns staying with Mom," he said.

"You mean each of us?"

"We'll have to come up with a schedule."

"Where will we sleep?" I asked. While my mother was in the hospital, we had arranged to have her house painted and renovated. The bedrooms, except for hers, and the two bathrooms were in complete disarray. Even my sister's old room, which had been used as a storage area for thirty-five years, was inaccessible. The apartment, which had been smothered by decades of smoking, would now be cleansed, removing the layers of nicotine embedded in the walls, the floors and the couches.

"We'll have to sleep with Mom in her bed," he said.

Oddly enough, none of us were concerned about sleeping with my mother. None of us were freaked out by the oedipal implications.

"We'll only do this for a few weeks," Frank added. The plan was to get her used to the idea of having a full-time attendant. This was merely an interim solution.

The first night that I came to my mother's apartment, she was still reeling from being in the hospital. Like a lion locked in a cage, she fumed and huffed, shouting demands and complaining about how the doctors were out to get her. Despite this, she was ambulating with the walker, moving on her own. And because of the oxygen tank and weeks of not smoking, her face now looked reddened with blood.

I had to talk over the television loudly playing *Family Feud*. The theme song seared my brain like an ambulance's siren.

"Could I lower the TV?"

"Could you what?"

I grabbed the remote control; she watched my fingers working the volume button.

"What are you doing?"

"I can't hear anything, Mom," I said, lowering the volume, now finally able to speak without feeling like I had a spike in my brain.

"Don't mess up the cable," she said, unable to take her eyes off of my hand holding the remote. The remote was my mom's umbilical cord to the world. While people came and went—her children, attendants, and workers fixing her house—the television was her companion and friend.

"Do you want me to make you coffee for tomorrow morning?" I asked, trying to find a safe topic.

"Get the pot," she commanded, pointing to the kitchen.

"This one?" I said, now standing over the stove, holding the pot.

"That one."

I started turning the top of the pot to remove the chamber that held the coffee grinds.

"Twist it to the right," she shouted at me from the living room table.

"I know how to wash a pot," I said. It was important that I held my own. She needed limits or she would have chewed me to bits and spit me out.

"Take the chamber out, then throw the coffee grinds in the garbage."

"Mom, please, you're annoying me. I don't need you to shout instructions to me on how to clean the coffee pot," I barked. Since she'd been in the hospital, she was dependent on people to do everything for her. Go to the bathroom. Wipe her ass. Walk across a room. Bring her coffee. Shop for her. Everything. It irritated her to be dependent. She was mad at the world, mad mostly at herself, but took it out on her four children. The doctors, therapists and attendants were collateral damage.

That night we went to sleep after the talk shows at about twelve o'clock.

My mother lay down, then turned on the oxygen machine. It snapped on with a jolt. It chugged and groaned, like a wounded dragon chained to the side of a mountain.

"Are you OK?" I asked.

"I'm fine," she said.

"Good night," I said.

Now I lay down next to her, sleeping in the same bed my father once slept in beside my mother twenty-five years ago. My mind flooded with images of my dad, images and emotions of living in this apartment, of how much noise the apartment could make with all of us in it. Christmas. Dinners at five o'clock, my parents demanding that everyone sit and eat at the same time. Holidays, some of them not so happy. Birthdays. Deaths.

I turned over onto my stomach. How could I possibly fall asleep? I could still smell smoke in the linen fabric, as if after all of these years the smoke merged at the molecular level, binding into the cotton fibers. I could hear my mother calling me a phony because I'd complained about her smoking since I'd quit twenty-two years ago.

I turned over and looked up at the ceiling.

Then, slowly, out of sheer exhaustion, I began to drift off.

I woke up at about two in the morning. I looked over to the other side of the bed. Mom was snoring from her open mouth, the oxygen cables trailing from her nose, her arms splayed out like Christ on the cross. Poor Mom.

I turned over, trying to sleep again. I felt sad. Sad for the twenty-five years she had lived alone after my father died. Then I felt angry at my dad for dying of cancer and leaving her to fend alone in the world. I felt angry at God for stripping her of her freedom, for subjecting her to being helpless.

The next few days, all four siblings called and texted each other. I called Camille. Frank called Lynn. Lynn called Camille. We never all talked together. We were all concerned about how to best help my mom without grinding ourselves and our families down. My mother finally got a bed for my old bedroom, so now we could all sleep in a separate bed. But my mom only wanted her four children to stay over. She didn't want a night attendant; she didn't even want her grandchildren to stay. This wasn't sustainable.

A few nights later, leaving my wife and kids at 8 p.m., I arrived at about ten to relieve the attendant. As I opened the door to the apartment, my ears were flooded with the blaring sounds of the television playing the theme song to *Family Feud*.

"Good evening," I said.

"What?"

"Please turn the television down."

"I can't hear you."

I took the remote and turned the television down.

"Sorry, Mom, I can't take the noise."

Before I got the television noise down, I heard, "Ding! The survey says..."

After I settled in, we sat down and talked. My mother had resumed drinking wine since she'd been home.

"I don't know what it is, I'm shaky in the morning; I'm afraid to get out of bed," she said, taking a sip from the wine glass.

"You've been through a lot of trauma," I said.

"That's what you people tell me. I must have been in bad shape in the hospital."

"You were in bad shape," I replied. I didn't say just how bad she was, that at points it felt like she was hanging by a thread.

"And with my cousin, Tutti, dying and now Jean," she added, "I feel like I'm looking in the face of death."

"I know, Mom, it must be very frightening." She used to babysit for Tutti when he was a kid. Now he was dead, and she was still above the earth. In the same week, Jean, her good friend of thirty years, had passed away suddenly from heart failure. She, Jean and Mary from work used to go out to drink, for dinners and shows. The fact is, except for her cousin Rosemary, almost all of her relatives were dead. She was the last one standing.

As we talked, I realized even though what my mom was asking for was irrational and not sustainable, it was what she needed. After sixty something years of sacrificing her life for her children—working, at times being the main bread winner, the steady, the rock—she needed the four of us. For so many of those years, it was my mother holding up the four of us, and yes, my father too. Like she had a ball and chain wrapped around her neck, she trudged through life, pushing us to do more, to do better, as the veins in her neck thickened and bulged. And now, from somewhere in the depths of her addled mind, she wanted us to do the same. This mighty little woman walked the earth for years with four children and a husband hung from her neck; now the four of us struggled to hold the weight of this same one little old lady.

15

Our Buried Caesars

I had just moved back to New York City from California. I was now living in Manhattan; it was like I was discovering NYC for the first time. Living in Oakland, a city where I didn't know anyone, taught me how to explore NYC and how to seek out new things, new experiences.

In my scouring of goings on in Manhattan, I found that there was a monthly meeting of Italian American writers at the Cornelia Street Cafe. It was a mix of featured and open mic readers. I was curious. What would Italian writers write about?

I went down that Saturday, open minded. Maybe I would make some friends. Learn something new.

There were a few featured readers who were spectacular. People like Victoria Repetto and Anthony Valerio. I now know that there were writers there I would get to know decades later. People like my friend George Guida. Funny to be sitting in a room with someone you'd only get to know twenty-five years later.

I was spellbound. Italian Americans writing about Italian American topics? About their loud families. Sunday dinners. Images of the crucified Christ. Malocchio pendants. Hard-working blue-collar families.

The host of the reading, and the president of the group, Bob Viscusi, read from his poem *An Oration Upon the Most Recent Death of Christopher Columbus.*

Bob was short, balding and thin. He looked like he could be related to Allen Ginsberg. He was very expressive. A terrific reader. He recited, cocking his head curiously, gesturing wildly with his arms.

> *i found christopher columbus hiding in the ashtray*
> *what are you doing there, if you please?*
> *no one smokes, he said, leave me alone.*

Watching and hearing Viscusi was like experiencing an opening in the galaxy. Not only was he a gifted writer and presenter of his work, but he also wrote about the things I grew up with. People arguing about which insurance they have, how you get to New Jersey from Queens. But he took these mundane topics and elevated them to a different cosmos. They were my concerns, but not just my concerns. They were so specific they were universal. I was exploding with revelation.

I took one of the flyers describing his next reading. This one at the Nuyorican Cafe in the East Village.

Again, Bob read from his poem *Columbus*, but also read excerpts from his novel *Astoria*. The prose in *Astoria* was sophisticated and insightful; it read like some mysterious combination of Dante, Robert Browning and Cicero. The sentences could go on for nearly a page, as if Bob was playing with you. In his inimitable way, Bob teased the reader, writing in the preface that his sentences read like the autobiography of a pinball. And indeed, the beautifully crafted prose caught you by surprise, often meandering into totally unexpected, but delightful, directions.

Despite the stylistic elements, *Astoria* was about growing up Italian American in Astoria, Queens. I grew up in Queens. How could that be an epic subject? Something worthy of being written about?

This was the beginning of my relationship with Bob.

Then, over the years, I saw Bob in Greenwich Village at readings and sometimes just randomly bumped into him on the street. He'd always ask me about the book I was reading or discuss the book he had in his hand. Our random rendezvous would extend into thirty-minute conversations in the street, or a quick sit-down coffee. We both had so much to say to each other. I was always eager to listen to Bob. He'd read so much, knew so much. Wrote several books. Not to mention that he was a professor of English literature.

Then, after some twenty-five years of knowing Bob, I moved to Midwood, near Brooklyn College, where he lived and taught. Bob told me that he had a stroke recently. He said that he was forgetting things. Bob wrote my number down countless times on napkins and pieces of paper, which he was never able to find.

Then he stopped remembering my name.

I would often call Bob to schedule getting together for a coffee or to eat.

Bob knew who I was every time I called. He knew my voice, though he'd often forget my name.

At coffee, we'd discuss literature, other Italian American writers. I got the inside scoop on the Italian American writers' community. Who Bob liked, who he didn't like.

When my manuscript *Call Me Guido* was accepted for publication, I asked Bob if he would write a blurb.

"It would mean so much to me," I said.

"Really?" he replied, very humbly.

"Bob, you're one of the reasons I write on Italian American themes. You've been an amazing influence on me."

Still, Bob seemed surprised.

"*Call Me Guido* is a ballsy title," he then added.

We then went to Bob's house. It was a big Victorian with a great porch on a dead-end street. Bob lived there with his wife, Nancy, whom I'd met on the street a few times. I'd never met Bob's two children, Victoria and Robert. They were only slightly younger than me.

As soon as I walked in the door, I saw the many bookcases packed with Italian and Italian American writers. Calvino. Vittorini. Eco. Anthony Valerio. It felt like I was in some clandestine laboratory where a part of my consciousness was incubated.

We then sat down in his lanai room near the piano. Bob started playing a bluesy rag-time piece, but then seemed to lose his way.

He turned around to look at me.

"I used to be very good. I can't remember anything anymore," he said.

"You're still good. I can hear that you know how to play."

"But I can't play the same."

Then I noticed that Bob was crying. Tears ran down his face. I put my hands on his hands.

"That's OK, Bob."

But this crying wasn't about playing piano. It was about his mind running away from him. Bob Viscusi's once great mind was now eluding its owner. *Where had the time gone?* Bob was asking. *Who was he now?* Sometimes, he was crystal clear and could recite poems and recall authors and their works. Sometimes, Bob was lost in the thread of a conversation.

We often met each other walking up the street that led to our homes. On one of these encounters, Bob invited me to an award ceremony at Brooklyn College for the work he'd done at the Wolf Institute for the Humanities. He was being honored with a lifetime award; it was a very big deal. The other professors praised him. What a giant intellect and great poet he was. A mind that inspired his professors and students. One professor said that what stood out about Bob when he first met him was he was a great dresser.

Then when Bob got up to give his thank you speech, he started reading from his papers. The audience was hushed, awaiting Bob's great words. Within only about a minute, Bob seemed to lose his way. He shuffled the papers, dropping one of them. It wasn't so much that people were shocked. These were his colleagues. They knew his situation. The silence that ensued was like a loving hug, as if everyone sitting in that room held Bob closely and then lifted him high up to the sky.

Since I lived near Bob, George Guida, having now met him at an Italian American writers' conference, said that he'd let me know when he was coming in to visit Bob. We could stop by his house together, go to dinner.

When we learned that Bob became suddenly even more ill, George and I made a visit to Lenox Hill Hospital to visit him.

Bob woke up when we walked in.

As usual, Bob asked all the questions. Even lying there, frail and tired, Bob's curiosity was still churning.

George pulled out his copy of Bob's *Buried Caesars* and read the preface.

The preface described how most non-Italians and even Italians are completely unaware of the depth of their history. Most people only see the Italian impact on music, culture, language and history from the head up. Buried beneath the surface is the deep history that is yet to be excavated.

"Bob, do you remember calling me to read versions of the preface?" asked George.

Bob nodded weakly, hardly able to project his voice.

This was all very touching. Hearing George read the preface reminded me of why Bob was so important in my own discovery of Italian American studies and literature. I'm doing the excavation that Bob was alluding to in *Buried Caesars.*

Finally, George read Bob's inscription on his copy of *Buried Caesars.*

To George, who perhaps will help me in deciding what to think of all of this.

That inscription sums up Bob's curiosity and contribution to Italian American studies. After achieving so much, writing several seminal books on Italian American literature, and influencing so many with his writing and charisma, Bob's note to George confirmed his own eternal curiosity.

Bob's note to George made it clear that, even after all these years, after reading and writing on Italian American subjects, we all have so much to learn about our buried Caesars.

16

Bigger Than U.S. Steel

"Can you come to Mom's today?" my sister Camille asks.

My eighty-six-year-old mother has been hospitalized three times in the past three years. Initially for breaking her vertebrae, then twice for breaking the same hip. In the wake of this, my brother Frank, my sister Camille, my other sister Lynn, and I are trying to figure out how to best take care of her.

"I have to figure out my schedule. Maybe I can squeeze in the train ride in between meetings and calls." I often work from my mom's place these days when I can manage a two-hour window to travel the distance from south Brooklyn to northeast Queens. I need the whole two hours in case there are service delays.

Camille is silent for a beat.

"You sound worried," I say. Between Camille, Lynn and Frank we're usually discussing schedules to take care of my mom, but there's something else going on now.

"Bob is sick," says Camille. "He's been coughing and has had a fever." Camille's husband, Bob, has been sick for a few weeks now and is getting worse. Two weeks ago, we would have thought that he had the flu or a cold.

"I don't know if I should go over to Mom's now," adds Camille, sighing.

I'm taking this in quietly. Thinking.

"What's his fever?" I ask.

"One hundred and one for a few days."

"Has he taken Tylenol?"

"And antibiotics."

"Is he coughing?"

"Constantly."

"Has he lost his sense of taste and smell?"

"Yes, why?"

"That's one of the symptoms of COVID."

"Please don't tell me this. I'm going to lose my mind."

I say that maybe I misread that somewhere.

"I'll come to Mom's today," I say, realizing the urgency. I'll have to rearrange my day and leave immediately.

As I walk to the subway, there are ambulances zooming back and forth on the street. Then on the train, I see more people wearing masks than just a few days ago.

When I get to my mom's place, I immediately walk over to the kitchen sink and wash my hands. Then I take the groceries out of the bag, one at a time and either wash them with disinfectant or wash them with soap in the sink.

"What are you doing?" my mother demands to know. My mom has always been stern, but in her present condition, she is mean. The person who took care of us all our lives has been swallowed by an extreme version of her former self. As if the fangs that she used to fight through this life are now biting back on her. This other person is sometimes nasty, rude, suspicious, and curt. Attributes we would never have previously associated with my mom.

"I need to wash everything down first," I say from the kitchen. I repeat myself a few times shouting over the blare of the television. She watches my every move cautiously.

"Are you crazy?" she asks in an irritated voice when I step into the living room, having washed everything. She continues talking but I can't hear her.

Now I ask her to lower the television. A game show is playing at full volume.

"You're such a pain in the ass," she says. I take the remote and put the television on mute.

"Do you know what's going on, Mom?"

"I know what's going on, but this is ridiculous."

The fact is she does not know what's going on. This is not the same sharp person she's always been. She doesn't read anymore. She watches "Family Feud," "The Price Is Right" and other game shows at lunatic volume levels. I visit to care for and spend time with her but have to argue about the television for the first ten minutes. Every time.

When I leave, I take the train home, now worried about Bob, hoping he'll be OK.

If Bob is infected, Camille might also be infected. And there is no reason to believe that I am not infected. Or Frank isn't infected. Or Lynn isn't infected. How can anyone know who is infected? No one can get tested. No one can get admitted to the hospital. How can we take care of my mom if any one of us is unknowingly infected?

And every day gets worse. More and more people start wearing masks on New York City streets. Everywhere. And the deaths pile up. In rapid succession, schools close, the lockdown is instituted. We are in full crisis mode. The news rushes over us like a dark cloud.

And now with Bob getting worse, and Camille getting more worried, we need to figure out who can visit my mom and when. We all agree to pause visiting her for at least two weeks just to know if any of us are infected.

And at this point we are not even sure if we can get a health aide to attend to my mom. People are told not to leave their houses unless they need to go to the store, get medical supplies or exercise. Everyone is scared of each other. You can see the fear in the faces of people on the streets. The masks only make people seem more menacing.

At home, the nights are now filled with the screams of ambulance sirens going all night. There are blue and red flashing ambulance lights blinking outside of our apartment almost every night. All night long.

My mom spends the next two weeks alone. Sometimes she answers the phone, sometimes she doesn't. I imagine my mom creeping from bed to chair using her walker, shackled to an oxygen tank. Her days and nights indistinguishable. Her only company a shrieking television resounding with the dings of game shows.

After two weeks, when I go to visit her, she doesn't answer the intercom. I use the key I have, just in case, to open the door.

As I walk in, I find her lying on the couch, her mouth wide open. With her chest rising and falling, I can tell that she's sleeping.

When she wakes up and sees me, her eyebrows wrinkle, not sure if she is dreaming me, or if I'm really there.

"Are you OK, Mom?"

"I'm a little confused," she says. There's no smile on her face. She looks pale and vacant. Somewhere in the back of her mind, she knows her children are always there for her. But I know at this moment, she's feeling abandoned. In my mother's current mental state, it's hard for her to grasp that the entire world is grappling with a pandemic. She forgets things people tell her. The news befuddles her. What's true and not true? And no one has ever seen anything like this before.

I take her oxygen level with the finger device she keeps near the television remote control. She guards them both like a snake protecting her eggs. When I try to take the oxygen monitor, she eyes me sharply, like I'm stealing it from her.

As I measure her oxygen level, she drifts in and out, her eyes opening and closing.

I use the oxygen monitor a few times to make sure of the reading. Her oxygen is dangerously low.

I call Camille.

"Her oxygen is at like seventy-five."

"What? My god. That's frightening."

My mother is very weak. I get her up to eat, but she almost immediately needs to lie down again.

We call the doctor, who prescribes prednisone and antibiotics, just to be sure. Perhaps she picked up the virus. She doesn't have the telltale symptoms, but she clearly isn't well. Her oxygen level has taken a dangerous dip.

"With the oxygen levels she's showing, she could have a sudden shut down of a vital organ," the doctor says. He explains that this is why her brain isn't working correctly.

After talking to the doctor, Camille tells me about a conversation she had with my mom a few days ago.

"Mom, we're nervous about seeing you."

"Would you rather kill me with the virus or kill me with loneliness?"

"Mom, that's a crazy question."

"No, I'm serious. I'd rather die of the virus than not see my children."

While my sister tells me the story, I imagine my mother, who is already unable to breathe due to seventy-plus years of smoking, being intubated. Alone in a hospital bed, hanging onto life by a thread.

As she speaks to my mother, Camille holds back her emotion; she cannot let my mom know how she feels at that moment. My mom has made us all tough-skinned, though her children all cry on the inside. Privately.

"What do you want me to do?" asks Camille.

"I want to see my children. I need to see you. I don't care if this damn thing kills me."

And so, we go to see my mom, risking everything to take care of her. To be with her. What other choice do we have?

In a few days, her oxygen level has gotten better. The color in her face returns. The scowl has been replaced by a sometime smile.

After spending the day with her, having made sure she eats and takes her pills, I help her to the couch. I have to go home now. Camille will stop by in an hour or so.

"I'm on the road to recovery," she says, unable to keep her eyes open. "I'm bigger than U.S. Steel," she adds, as she falls asleep.

"Love you, Mom," I say, laughing, as I close the door.

There is no reply. She is already sleeping.

17

Disappearing into Letters

"You should always write the truth," said David.

"What if it hurts someone?" I asked.

"Don't worry about hurting anyone, whether it's your mailman, your doctor, or your mother."

"That sounds terrifying."

"Your work should read like it's forbidden," he said.

Our friendship began with emails back and forth, then launched into something very deep and personal. There was a period when David was like a father to me. And now we have ceased to exist for each other as flesh and bone; we are letters on a page, notes back and forth. With all his flaws, my father never left my side, even in death. David, however, has been reduced to the gray mist of words.

After I had read David's *Toughguys*, I wrote to him, saying that I loved his book. It brought me back to the world of my father, I said. He wrote back almost immediately, saying that he often received notes like this from readers. The book, based on the life of Jimmy Roselli, the crooner, touched something in the psyche of Italian Americans, David said. And he was right, Roselli was a link to the past, back to our fathers and mothers, back to their immigration and assimilation. Roselli didn't sing in standard Italian; he sang in Neapolitan dialect. For Italian Americans this was very special; this was their private language, a language that even their own countrymen didn't always understand, not to mention Anglo-Americans. Roselli was so loved, he made the mobsters, their wives, and their mothers weep. According to the story, Roselli wasn't cowed by the mob. He demanded payment for every performance and every piece of music. And yet they didn't kill him. They couldn't kill him. *Toughguys* was also the kind of book, concerned with gangsters and Mafia, that I would never have read previously. But my father's death, now fifteen years past, began to call to me, drawing me to imagine the world he grew up in, the world he knew. If I could listen to the music he liked and read the books he would have read, perhaps I could conjure him, like a genie in a bottle. I could make him manifest. I read *The Valachi Papers, Boss of Bosses*, and *Underboss: Sammy the Bull Gravano's Story of Life in the Mafia*. In my feverish research, I stumbled on *Toughguys*.

My father often said that Roselli sang "in the real Neapolitan dialect," as if to impress me. As if I cared. What kid likes his parents' music? And my father was fascinated by gangsters like John Gotti and Paul Castellano. He'd grown up in downtown Manhattan and personally knew people like this. His first cousin married the daughter of Joey "Beck" DiPalermo. My mother recalled meeting Joe Beck, saying that he dressed impeccably and was incredibly cordial. He was well spoken and charming. But he was a vicious murderer. And despite his thirty years in prison, his daughter denied reports in the paper describing the brutal killings, saying they were all lies.

While my father didn't aspire to be like Joe Beck, he had a respect for the power Joe Beck wielded. And I'm sure he envied Joe Beck's lavish lifestyle, expensive clothes and gorgeous cars. But for me the Mafia was as shameful as my father's gambling and the chaos and desperation it caused in our family. I associated gambling with Mafia and Mafia with murder.

Soon after our initial correspondence, David and I began writing back and forth feverishly. We mostly wrote about music and literature. Then, after a few months, we agreed to meet at a restaurant near the Writers Room, off Broadway.

I was in the café when David entered. I got up to shake his hand; I'd recognized him from the book-sleeve picture. He was very short and wiry in person and wore a horrible toupee. He didn't look like a guy who would be fascinated with tough guys.

"No one's ever written a book like this," he said, speaking like his jaws were wired closed, his teeth almost always touching, like he'd been a boxer. He didn't speak like a tough guy; he spoke like someone who'd grown up in Queens in the 1950s.

"What made you interested in Roselli?" I asked, timidly. I wanted to handle this encounter tenderly. I needed to get to know David.

"I heard Roselli at a restaurant and couldn't believe how marvelous he was," said David. "I asked the waiter who the singer was. I had to get to know his music." David looked at you from the corner of his eye, with a hint of suspicion. He spoke too confidently, belying his insecurity. Maybe he wondered if you knew he was wearing a rug. You could see his mind wriggling behind his eyes. He wasn't handsome, by any means. He wore a long gold rope chain that hung on his neck reminding you of the tough guys he wrote about. The gold chain was visible when his shirt was open. Unless he showed you, you wouldn't see the Star of David that weighed the chain down like an anchor.

David could tell I was serious about music. I'd read his books on other Italian crooners, like Bobby Darin. And I'd read books on Sinatra, Coltrane, and Miles. I wasn't like the small-time singers who hoped David would write a book about them. Or the following of Italian Americans who reminisced about Roselli and his bygone era. David had given their hero recognition and they were immensely loyal to him. While I wasn't looking for those things, I *was* looking for my father. I had an agenda, too.

Our first meeting ended politely. We then resumed our correspondence. At the time, he was finishing his book on Tony Bennett. It will be the best book available on Tony Bennett, he crowed. I'm looking forward to reading it, I wrote back. There weren't any good books available about Tony Bennett, it was true, I said. They were either too superficial or too fawning. I'd come across these books as I was writing short comic pieces about the crooners and had been hungrily in search of ideas, sources, anything I could get my hands on.

David and I started to meet socially. We'd go out for a drink in Little Italy, or downtown Manhattan near the Writers Room. I showed him some of my writing. I had a collection of short comic stories about historical figures. Freud and Jung, more obsessed with haberdashery than their ideas. Filippo Brunelleschi, who grew his nose with magic potions so he'd win the commission to build the cupola for the Santa Maria del Fiore in Florence. The last story I showed him, perhaps out of place, was about my father's death.

"I read your stories," said David, sitting at a café near the Writers Room. I was afraid to hear his response. He'd hate them. I waited for him to say something, blinking nervously.

"I liked the one about your father."

"Really?" I asked. I was embarrassed about that story. It made mention of my father's gambling and our family's humiliation in dealing with its consequences.

"That's your first great story," he said. "But you need to work on it," he paused. "Your love for your father and your father's dedication to you comes through," he said. "It makes your honesty about his gambling more powerful."

Hearing "that's your first great story" had a strong effect on me. On the one hand, it seemed pathetic that at forty years old, I had only one story. On the other hand, I had at least one great story. One great one.

"What about the other stories?" I asked

"You should write about your father. That's where your stories are." When discussing writing, David didn't mince words. He didn't try to make you feel better, or worse. He was very matter of fact. Discussing writing was like a doctor discussing your health. You had to know if you had a disease. You couldn't remain in the dark.

"What about the other stories?" I asked again.

"The other stories weren't very good," he said.

"Writing about my family feels strange," I said.

"Write about what's embarrassing," replied David. "Write about what makes you uncomfortable." Writing about my family felt like I was a snitch telling our secrets, talking about our shame in public. Especially stories about my father and his gambling and its destructive impact on our lives—on my mother. I had a hard time talking to my therapist privately about these things, much less writing stories with the intent of people reading them.

"Do you have more stories about your father?"

"I do," I said. "I have other stories about my family too."

"Show me those. Send me the manuscripts. I'll read them and give you some suggestions."

In this gesture, it was as if some plate tectonics of my mind had shifted, upending the solid ground and setting the ghost of my father loose in my blood. I discovered that writing about my father made me sad. It was as if I could feel a part of me melting, turning into a puddle in front of me, a puddle that reflected my own image. But while it was painful and confusing, it was also healing. Releasing these long-held feelings freed me from their hold.

And I had finally found someone who believed in my work. Someone who could elevate my writing. A teacher. I found David in the search for my father. And while my father wasn't interested in literature, he was the first prototype of a literary tragic figure for me. My father was a fallen man, someone who looked up into the face of humiliation. Despite this, or maybe because of this, you couldn't help but experience his enormous humanity. His suffering made him vulnerable, loving, kind, and understanding. If there's honesty in my writing, it's from my father's inescapable confrontation with reality. Our whole family was trapped in my father's gambling predicament from the third-floor project apartment facing the Department of Sanitation's garbage trucks.

After I sent David my work we met again at the café.

He handed me back my manuscripts, with his notes on them.

"You see here," he said after I'd read the comments, "you're edit-orializing here, and here," now pointing to another section on the page. "You're repeating yourself." His comments immediately made sense. I don't think anyone's criticism ever resonated so well with me before. "Now here," he continued, "we don't believe you. Would you ever say that?" he asked. I don't remember the sentence, but it's true I would never have said something quite like what I'd written. "Write simply. Write like you would say it."

"I don't know if I can do this anymore," he said one day, a few months later. "You know I have students."

"Oh, of course," it suddenly occurred to me. "I should pay you for this," I said. "I'm sorry."

"Don't be sorry."

"Please, just tell me how much I should pay you." I wish he had told me this up front.

We sorted out the details. I'd mail him my manuscripts and he'd make comments and then we'd meet and discuss them. It was very fair. And we enjoyed the time we spent together. We started to joke around and have laughs together. Talking and writing about my father evoked my father's spirit. His being even seemed to mingle with David's. David would sign his emails to me "Love, David." He'd ask about my mother, make sure I gave her his regards. He seemed enamored of my mother. She represented something mythical to him. She was an Italian mother, something he'd written about and knew in theory.

He would sometimes call me up to help him with computer relat-ed things, like how to find information on the internet. It was like we were both father and son to each other.

A few weeks later he called me at midnight.

"Hello?"

"It's David, sorry it's late."

"That's OK."

"I just thought of the title for the story you sent me about your son."

"Yeah."

"It's called 'Separation,'" he said.

"That's perfect."

"Of course it is" he said. "You have to work on your titles. They're terrible." Then he hung up. The important thing here is that he cared about me, like a father would care about a son. He was looking after me, like my father did.

After a while, he'd write or call me just to ask if I was writing.

"Write every day, even if it's just a little bit."

"I'm trying."

"Write about your father, your family. That's where your stories are."

I was writing nearly every night now, sometimes writing on my mobile phone on the way to work meetings and back. I was making progress.

During one of our rendezvous, David told me that *Toughguys* was being optioned by a movie producer. The problem, he said, was that he needed a screenwriter to turn the book into a screenplay.

"But I don't know anybody I trust."

"I have a friend who is a screenwriter," I said.

"Who is he?"

"Ric Menello," I said. "He directed the Beastie Boys videos, then went on to write and ghostwrite screenplays. He co-wrote the screenplay for *Two Lovers* and some other films."

David listened. His forehead and eyebrows twitched.

"He's also from the world Roselli knew. He grew up in Brooklyn, comes from an Italian family. He knows more about film than anyone I've ever met."

David fidgeted, folding a napkin as I spoke.

"We're always talking about film," I said. "I see him at the café near my house."

"Is he going to cost me a fortune?"

"I don't know about that," I said. "Ric doesn't strike me as the expensive type." When I saw Ric on the streets, he would agree to hang out with me if I bought him a pizza, or a seltzer. He wasn't begging. And most of the time I offered.

"But what do I know," I said. "That's between you two."

After they met a few times and talked, Ric was hired to write the screenplay.

As if preparing Ric for writing David's screenplay, we arranged viewings of old foreign movies at my place. *Salvatore Giuliano, The Earth Trembles, Christ Stopped at Eboli*, and other films Ric recommended. He knew the back stories of each film, how they were financed, the directors' personal lives.

During that time, I was reading David's books of short stories. The stories were beautifully written and powerful, but extremely sad. Some of the stories were autobiographical, revolving around his wife, Lana, who was an alcoholic. Having carried Lana, completely unconscious, out of our apartment after one of our film viewings, I knew the severity of her drinking. David was so angry at Lana, he wouldn't even help me carry her into a taxi. He only cursed and fumed. At one film viewing, Lana arrived, her cheeks and forehead tinted blue, from having fallen flat on her face.

David began pushing Ric very hard to complete the screenplay. He called me up to complain about Ric.

"The guy's terrific," said David, "but he's got to stick to the deadline. I can't have this thing drift out into forever." His criticisms of Ric had a tinge of cruelty. All David cared about was that damned screenplay; he didn't care if it killed Ric to race to the finish. Nothing would ever stand between David and his work, I came to know.

Then the time finally came for a reading of an early draft of the screenplay.

As Ric read, I could hear that he filled David's story with the characters and voices of his own family and people he knew. Ric wrote with the blood of his uncles and cousins to make the story real. By the end of the reading, Ric was sullen and quiet. David didn't notice this or didn't care. When David got up to go to the bathroom, Ric sighed, saying, "Please tell David I had to go." Revisiting the world of his family, most of whom were dead and gone, had taken the life out of him. I knew how he felt. He gave me a hug before I closed the door.

Later, David called me and asked me to attend a conference at the City University of New York. He was on a panel of readers that included James Kaplan, who wrote *Frank: The Voice*, about Frank Sinatra.

After the reading, David introduced me to Kaplan. Kaplan was well dressed and handsome, unlike David. He wore a business suit and tie. He was cocky.

They started to discuss their respective subjects.

"Sinatra and Bennett are two different kinds of Italians," said Kaplan. "Sinatra was half Genoese and half Sicilian. Bennett's family was from Bari. Very different types." It sounded like they were talking about breeds of dogs. I didn't say anything, though I didn't like the comment.

David wasn't Italian but he was interested in the history of Italian American immigration. *Toughguys* was prefaced by the unique story of how Italians came to America, how they were received by the Anglo-Americans of the time. He had taken up the cause of Italian Americans. I learned that David felt this gave him license to make racist comments about Muslims.

In talking about 9/11 and the horrible attack on the World Trade Center, he went on a rant about Arabs and Muslims.

"They're animals, the Arabs."

"I don't agree with you," I said.

"What other group would do something like that?" he asked.

"The Middle East is a political mess that America helped to create. It's not the people or the religion."

"I support the Italians, don't I?" he asked.

"Yes, but what does that have to do with anything?"

"You should support me on my position. You don't know enough about Israeli-Arab history. You couldn't understand it."

"I know enough about it to know that it's always right to promote humanism and fairness."

"You don't know anything."

"How would you feel if I stood by and listened to someone saying anti-Semitic things? Wouldn't you expect me to speak up?"

At this point, David lost all patience with me. He apparently felt that I didn't understand the issue. He thought that his having a genuine interest in the history of a humiliated population meant that I'd support his heaping humiliation on another population, out of loyalty. My father would never ask something like that from me.

Months later, Ric died of a sudden heart attack. Ric was overweight, ate poorly, and in general didn't take care of himself. When I heard he was ill, I ran to the hospital to see him. The front desk pointed me to his room. When I ran in, I found him on a hospital bed, his head leaning back, his mouth wide open.

"He just died a few moments ago," the attendant said, and apologized for not warning me in advance. When I approached Ric's body, it was as if the last breath of air had just been expelled from his body. Like his last breath was still in the air.

At the hospital, I met Ric's cousin Vinny and his uncle Pat, as if they stepped out from the pages of *Toughguys*. It was like I knew them already. I'd already heard their voices and gestures in Ric's readings. And they reminded me of my own family.

Some months later David asked to borrow money so he could take a trip to California. He needed to go out west to interview some people for his in-progress book on Woody Allen. I gave him the money without question. Instead of paying me back, I suggested that he read one of my manuscripts. We calculated the number of pages that equaled the money I'd loaned him.

Months after David read my manuscripts, I sent him and a few other friends a draft of a story I was excited about. I can't remember the story. I'd often send drafts to friends to read, if they had time. When I sent a draft like this, I wasn't asking for editing assistance, or proofing. Just immediate responses. Does the story make sense? Does it feel like a story? A few of my friends wrote back about the story. David wrote back that he'd already delivered services in full for the money I'd loaned him. I wrote back saying I only asked him to read it if he had time. He wrote back, ignoring my note, saying that his reading of my work was serious business, unlike the efforts of my other friends, who were not serious writers. I'm a professional editor, he added. I was editor of the *Paris Review*, taught writing at the University of Toronto and the New School. His comments were biting and harsh and seemed completely out of place. The back and forth on this churned my stomach. I apologized profusely, though I wasn't sure exactly what I had apologized for.

Over the next few months, our email dialogue almost ceased. Now and again, I'd receive a forwarded email from David regarding a journal that was accepting a submission. His emails to me were no longer signed "Love, David."

I continued to send David notes to pass along articles I thought he might like to read. And now my writing was getting published.

On one occasion, I sent him a note regarding a recently published story of mine. He wrote back asking if I'd read an email he had sent. I then recalled an email David had sent that was forwarded to a number of people. It wasn't addressed to me and, as I was travelling, I forgot to read it. When I apologized to David and told him I was travelling and had missed his email, he wrote back, "That's not how this works." He was apparently upset that I'd missed his note to me. I read the article and responded. Whatever father and son relationship we'd known had now dissolved into thin air. We had unloved each other.

We've since written back and forth, sometimes about books we've read or music we've listened to. I've signed my letters "I miss you." I know I can't write him asking him about what happened, it would be too complicated. I get the feeling he'd either write an angry toxic reply or just completely deny everything. He'd say he'd been busy and that I was reading between the lines.

I think sometimes maybe I could ask him if my titles have improved. I've asked a number of times about getting together; it's just embarrassing to ask at this point. It's ironic that in searching for my father, I found David. And then David encouraged me to write my way back to my father. To bring him back to life. And while I've lost David, I have more of my father than I ever did.

18

Family Tree

Once again, my father-in-law, Richard, asks me when I'm going to send him information on my family's genealogy.

"My mother doesn't have the documents," I say. I've asked my mother a few times and she doesn't seem to be able to locate her mother's or father's birth certificate. She's eighty-five and is more concerned about walking steadily from the couch to the kitchen than family genealogy.

"If you have her parents' birth certificates, can't you look up their parents' birth information?"

It's like he doesn't hear me. As if all families have that information readily at hand. As if all families care about that kind of thing. We weren't raised to venerate our family history. Maybe there's a reason in our case. Unlike Richard, my mother and father didn't receive an inheritance. They weren't bequeathed homes and antiques. The only thing my father left me when he died was his frayed boxer shorts and drawing notebooks.

But he asks me again.

"My mom doesn't know where those documents are."

At this point, Richard retells me again about his family history which extends back to sixteenth-century Germany, with a few English decedents thrown in, too. They have names like Frederic, Carl and Hermann. He's shown me the genealogical chart that he prepared from research he did along with research he paid for. The German names look beautiful, especially alongside the cities from which they hailed. Cities like Hamburg, Leipzig and Heidelberg.

While Richard talks about the majesty of his lineage, I, however, fantasize that they were scoundrels. That they stole money from poor people to accumulate their family riches. I picture miserly landowners shaking even the gold teeth from their hapless renters.

"Karl Wilhelm married Joanne Hess in Leipzig in 1625," he continues, now showing me the chart printed on a long scroll of papers pieced together.

I almost feel guilty that I don't have any information, as if my family is hiding something. I've now become curious to know more about my family history. It would be funny to produce a list of miscreants, rapists and half-wits for him to hang next to his family's genealogical chart. Then I could say, *"See now, we should have left well enough alone, right? But no, you had to dig up the dead, you had to make me exhume these reprobate cadavers from out of the ground where they had sunk in obscurity. Now we both have to imagine how my corrupt genes will show up in your grandchildren."*

But I don't say these things out loud. Instead, I compose myself. For the tenth time I repeat the bit of history that I know.

"You know that when my grandparents' parents left Southern Italy, they were fleeing poverty," I say.

I don't say that Southern Italians were lucky if they were merely worked to death. The ones that couldn't find steady work were starved to death. Maybe their wives were raped by the landowner. This was a legal practice on the books allowing this. Many were run out of the country, like criminals. This is evidenced by the mass exodus Southern Italy experienced before the turn of the 20th century.

I don't say that people like my grandparents may have slept on the fields where they worked, after toiling in the Southern sun all day. Travelling back and forth cost money. Their employers wouldn't house them. They were filthy animals, after all. And unlike animals, they were worthless. They slept without blankets, lying like dead things in the dark fields, their skin crawling with bugs and rodents.

I don't say that if the workers ate actual food, they ate molded bread, chewed on by mice. Otherwise, they drank water with salt, as if it were food. I don't say that Southern Italy had very few doctors and hardly any medicine. That the North consumed all of the monies and resources, leaving the South without infrastructure, without schools or proper roads.

In part because he probably would agree, I don't say that the North considered Southerners to be racially inferior and primitive. I don't go on too much because I would seem angry, which I'm not. Well, yes, I am. I also know that whatever I said, he would hear only his own thoughts, that he would read to me his genealogy and pontificate on the greatness of his lineage.

I imitate Richard's interrogations with a routine I've developed for my wife, Ainsley.

Speaking in German accent, I pound a fist into my other hand, saying "You must show me your identity papers to prove that you are not of an inferior race." I wrap my lips over my teeth, then hold my hands together behind my back and begin pacing and shouting like a Nazi officer. Ainsley laughs. She knows her father is insensitive and incapable of imagining any perspective that isn't his. She's had to live with him all of her life.

The truth is, I've come to like Richard. He can't help being completely blind to other people's misfortunes.

Richard isn't my father and I'm not his son. I'm his daughter's husband. Richard doesn't discuss feelings or thoughts. He's an engineer. He talks about how things work. How to fix a vacuum cleaner. How he reconstructed the front porch.

My father was a very different person. My father's gambling troubles and the trauma it caused our family forced him to stand naked before all of us. My father spoke like a man who'd been to war, who lived through tragedy. Ironically, my father's failures made him vulnerable and compassionate.

So, I push off Richard's questions about research into my family tree. Later in life maybe I'll look into this. My father's cousin said that she learned that our family name is associated with artisans from the North. Imagine that. It would be so great to know that they were luthiers, or composers who created art for the King's court.

But what I know is that our immediate ancestors came from Sicily and near Naples. They came to this country very poor. I can see them on a boat, looking out at the Statue of Liberty, dressed in rags, and whistling the theme of *The Godfather* as the ship turned into Ellis Island.

19

Proud Sorrow

If I know anything about Italian film, it's because I learned it from my friend, Ric Menello. And the more I came to learn about the films Ric loved, the more I came to know Ric.

I met Ric Menello at Vox Pop, an art café in Brooklyn, in about 2006. Balding, wearing thick glasses, Ric looked a little wild, like maybe he was crazy. But when Ric spoke, you listened. His knowledge of film and even of literature was encyclopedic. It was like Ric knew something about everything.

The night I met him he was showing Roberto Rossellini's *Rome, Open City* at Vox Pop, which I hadn't yet seen. Ric curated the film series at Vox Pop. This was one of his favorite films.

"Are you here to see *Rome, Open City?*" Ric asked, greeting me as I walked into the café. I shook my head no. I had actually come to meet a friend.

But I asked what was playing, out of curiosity. Ric gladly told me.

"Do you know what *Rome, Open City* is about?" Ric asked, scratching his beard as he spoke, narrowing his eyes. Ric was a portly man. He often looked disheveled, wearing shirts with stains on them and pants with tears. To be honest, he looked like a homeless person.

I said I didn't.

"It's about fear," he continued, in his strong Brooklyn accent. Like watching the film was dangerous. "It's about Italy's need to confess its sins to the world." As Ric spoke, he rocked back and forth, like he was praying.

"Italians are a very guilt-ridden people," said Ric.

I nodded, listening. Though Ric was intense, his eyes were heavy and sad.

"I should know," he added, now smiling, his black bushy Groucho Marx eyebrows arched across his eyes. "I'm Italian."

He continued, "Rossellini didn't have Fellini's cinematographic eye or De Sica's skill to translate the ordinary into something holy. Rossellini's films portrayed defeated people in vulnerable circumstances. And despite their poverty and vulnerability, Rossellini's characters stood for what they believed—even in the face of death."

"How do you know so much about film?" I asked, truly interested now to know who this person was.

"I went to NYU's film school," said Ric, wincing over his glasses. He often spoke like it hurt him to talk. "I've also directed some music videos and other crap," he sighed, understating his background. I would later learn that Ric directed the Beastie Boys' "You Gotta Fight" and "No Sleep till Brooklyn." He then wrote a few screenplays with James Gray. He was also an advisor to a number of directors who viewed Ric as a film historian and expert. They'd call or email him for advice. Ric was Hollywood's secret weapon. The funny thing is, I didn't learn all of this in full until after knowing Ric for a number of years.

Then I'd see Ric at Vox Pop and on Cortelyou Road, wandering the streets. I'd often run into him when I was with my then ten-year-old son, Theo. After picking up Theo from school, we'd go to eat at Vox Pop. And Ric would be sprawled out at a table, writing in his notebook.

One day, at the beginning of the school year, we met Ric at Vox Pop.

"How are you?" he asked Theo, exhaling, like seeing my son took an enormous existential weight off his shoulders. "School good?" Theo looked at me before answering. At ten years old, he didn't yet know what to make of Ric. Theo knew that Ric wasn't like other people.

"Do you like cowboy films?" Ric asked. Theo said yes. "You should watch *Rio Bravo* with your father. It's one of the great all-time films." Ric knew how to engage Theo. And he knew that if he wanted to talk to me, he had to include my son in the conversation. And Ric and I wanted to talk to each other. We'd come from Italian families, grew up and out of the same borough neighborhoods.

If I saw Ric on Cortelyou, I'd ask him to hang out. He'd say that he'd hang out if I bought him a pizza, which of course I did. If Ric had made money with the success he'd had, he certainly didn't have any now. I didn't realize until much later the extent of Ric's issues, that he had suffered from a deep depression. That he had serious bouts of mental illness.

When I did music performances at Vox Pop, I would call Ric and ask him to come.

"You know our deal, right?" he'd ask.

"I'll buy you all of the seltzer you'd like," I'd say. Ric didn't drink alcohol. Ric would position himself right at the front of the audience and stomp and clap when I played "Me and My Uncle."

Since we lived in the same neighborhood, we wound up spending a good amount of time together. We didn't have to call each other, for the most part.

During this time, I had been developing a friendship with a writer, David, who had written a book called *Toughguys*. *Toughguys* is a great story. It's about Jimmy Roselli, a singer contemporary of Frank Sinatra who refused to be cowed by the Mob. Instead, he made them weep with his beautiful and authentic singing style. And he sang in the Neapolitan dialect, which made him even more emotionally necessary to Italians like my father and apparently Ric's uncles and relatives, too. I had written to David after reading his book; we corresponded, then met. When David told me he'd been looking for someone to write the screenplay to *Toughguys*, I thought of Ric.

"Can he write this screenplay?" asked David. After all, *Toughguys* was his baby. He wouldn't work with just anyone.

"I know him from the neighborhood," I said. "Ric wrote the screenplay for *Two Lovers*, among other things. Also, he grew up in Brooklyn. He knew the people you write about in *Toughguys*. Look, meet with him. See if you think he's a good fit."

I received a call after they met.

"Where did you meet this guy?" David asked me. "He's amazing." Apparently, David and Ric really hit it off. They agreed to work together.

While Ric was writing the screenplay, we agreed that he and David would come over to my house to watch Ric's suggested films, as if we were all preparing Ric to write the screenplay.

When we watched *Mafioso*, starring Alberto Sordi, Arielle, my wife, made a ravioli dish she learned from a Sicilian cookbook I had bought.

"This is the most delicious ravioli I ever ate," said Ric, slurping as he ravenously scarfed down his food, rocking back and forth.

I shoved more from the bowl into his plate.

"Delicious," he repeated, pointing at the ravioli with his fork.

While we ate, we were also preparing my then two-year-old son, Travis, for bed. This time, Travis had just come out of the shower and bolted naked across the living room.

"Look at Travis," said Ric, "he's like a little wild man."

Ric loved coming to our house. It made him feel at home. Many people in our neighborhood treated Ric like he was the guy who directed the Beastie Boys. But to us, he was a family friend. Ric returned the warmth he received by being incredibly thankful and kind. Our family reminded him of his family, and he took great comfort in this. The fact is my entire relationship with Ric was built around him knowing my sons and my wife.

Over that summer we watched several films, accompanied by Ric's commentary. Among his favorites were *Salvatore Giuliano*, *Hands Over the City* and *Christ Stopped at Eboli* by Francesco Rosi, *Variety Lights* by Alberto Lattuada and *Il Generale Della Rovere* by Rossellini.

Then, after about six months, Ric asked if he could read a draft of the screenplay for *Toughguys* aloud. This time, our friend Angela, an aspiring screenplay writer, also joined us.

We served meatloaf that night. "This the best meatloaf I've ever had," said Ric, scarfing his food with gusto.

"Wait, that's what you say about my meatloaf!" said Angela. We all laughed.

After we ate, Ric began reading the screenplay. Ric infused the stories with characters out of his own life. I'd heard him talk about an uncle who sang on the same bill with Roselli. Ric's uncle became one of the characters in a scene. Ric imitated the voices and speech of the characters. You could tell that reading the story reminded him of family he missed. When he finished reading, we all sat silent. Angela wiped the tears from her face. David got up to go to the bathroom.

"Tell David I said goodnight," said Ric, shaking my hand as he walked out the door.

"Are you OK?" I asked.

"I'm just tired," said Ric, but I knew it was more than that. He'd been talking about the world he grew up in, the family he loved that were now all gone. He buried them in the story. I knew how he felt because I felt the same way.

Not long after the screenplay was finished, Ric suddenly died of a heart attack. Although he wasn't a healthy person, it took us all by surprise.

At his wake, my wife read a poem I wrote for Ric—I was afraid to read it and cry in front of everyone. Debi Ryan, the owner of Vox Pop, walked up to Ric's casket, broke a muffin in pieces and spread it on top of Ric's body. It was shocking. She turned around to face everyone.

"Now, this is the Ric I know," she said. And she was right.

Then Tom Martinez, a friend in the neighborhood, who also happened to be a Unitarian minister, got up to speak and read from *The Velveteen Rabbit*. He quoted from the scene where the Skin Horse is telling the Rabbit about how you become real.

"You become. It takes a long time. That's why it doesn't happen often to people who break easily, or have sharp edges, or who have to be carefully kept. Generally, by the time you are Real, most of your hair has been loved off, and your eyes drop out and you get loose in the joints and very shabby. But these things don't matter at all, because once you are Real you can't be ugly, except to people who don't understand."

At this, everyone at the wake was in tears. This quote encapsulated what we all knew about Ric. Ric didn't look or act perfect. But he was always real. Ric could make you laugh, but he also knew the sadness you felt. He had that insight. Watching the Italian neorealist films, growing up with people who watched them, from a culture that allowed you to be sad, to cry, and to show weakness, made Ric a person of enormous feeling and emotion. We felt his sadness, but he didn't weigh it down on us. Ric was proud. He didn't want everyone to know his issues, though we all knew he had serious issues. Instead, he smiled and joked. Finally, we knew Ric's sadness because he knew ours.

20

The Pig Doctor

My boss Scott held the status document up, blocking my view of his face, firing several questions which I couldn't answer or answered incorrectly. He was probably laughing at me, but he feigned anger. He didn't want me to see his face.

"You're making big assumptions here. I don't think you fully understand the problem," he said.

I didn't reply to his comment.

"What will you do when a new charge is developed? How will you disseminate it to the other agencies?"

Again, no answer.

I evaporated off the chair, like a mist.

I had learned in my travels across the desert the magical art of being invisible. Yes, I would be invisible, and Scott would not be able to see me. He would ask me a question and I would vanish into the air like Geronimo. The Apaches were known for their ability to skillfully hunt their victims, both human and animal. They'd contort their bodies into the position of tree or boulder nearly breathless, waiting. Like an afternoon shadow they'd creep on a deer and before the deer bent down again to nibble on a leaf, *whammo,* it was slaughtered by an arrow through the eyeball.

Perhaps Scott perceived that I was attempting to be invisible. Perhaps he had sensed that I was a medicine man.

I'm here, I'm gone. I'm here, I'm gone. Now I'm a raven flying over a canyon. Now I'm a rattlesnake. Could he see the dappled reds of a California sky streaking across my eyeballs?

As I sat there, unable to focus on anything, hoping I would disintegrate, I remembered an episode from a book that I'd read years ago called *Christ Stopped at Eboli* by Carlo Levi. Levi was deemed a threat to Mussolini's vision of Italy, and he was therefore banished to Gagliano, an obscure and poor village in Southern Italy. What could be worse than being sent to the backward arid land of Southern Italy, where the only porcelain toilet bowl in the village was thought of as more of a holy altar than a place to defecate?

In the book, there is an episode depicting the rounds the Pig Doctor would make to the village. When the village pigs have reached the appropriate level of procreation, the villagers select certain pigs to be relieved of their reproductive organs so they can fatten them. The meat from such pigs is tender and plentiful.

The Pig Doctor is as much a priest as he is a surgeon. The villagers are awed by his ability to remove the genitalia without killing or fatally injuring the pigs. Everybody has got to be good at something, right?

The village women line up, holding their pigs by ropes.

The pigs meanwhile squeal and whine, pulling on the rope, trying to make a last-minute dash, as if knowing the coming danger. They fear the Pig Doctor.

As he sharpens his knives, laying them out along with various scalpels and other accoutrements, the wail of the pigs increases.

The first pig is brought to him. Like a champion wrestler, he instantly pins the pig to the ground, and the owner helps tie the pig's legs and arms to pins bolted in the soil.

Baring its belly, the pig's eyes widen in horror.

In the case of a female, the Pig Doctor opens the pig with one upward tear and reaches in its body. He finds the string of flesh that leads to her ovaries. Having found those, he pulls one hand over the other, like a fisherman. Once the ovaries are exposed, he cuts them and tosses them to the dogs that are standing nearby, awaiting a midday snack. Almost as instantly he sews the belly back up and sends the demoralized pig on its way, limping.

The males are easier. The testes are easy to find and, without splitting open the pig, the testicles are thrown to the snarling dogs in seconds.

Everyone is delighted by the Pig Doctor's magic; everyone except the pigs who linger afterwards in a state of shock, unsure of what has just happened to them, sensing that it will only get worse.

Scott was the inevitable Pig Doctor. There was no escaping. No amount of carping, squealing, mewling, or squirming would make a difference. It didn't matter that I'd been to Pikes Peak, or that Felicia called me Rocky. Once Scott had you by the balls in one swift movement, he'd snip them off, leaving you to roil in pain, as he moved onto his next victim.

Coming out of my daydream, I looked at Scott again. Perhaps behind the paper he held to his face was a cutting knife.

21

The Short Long Man

In the neighborhood, they called my godfather "But But Benny" because he frequently said *but but* when he spoke or replied to a question. Benny was my godfather, but he was also a bookie for a notorious mobster, John Gotti. Benny lived a few blocks from the Ravenite Social Club on Mulberry Street where Gotti held court. They were friends. Unlike Gotti, Benny wasn't a murderer. And he wasn't a braggart or showy. Benny was loved by his children and wife and he was good to my mother and father. And he was funny. I have only good memories of him.

Benny had been a longshoreman or as I used to say, a Short Long Man. I called him a Short Long Man, not because, like so many of my mother's Sicilian relatives, he was short and squat, but because I liked the way Short Long Man sounded.

But for as long as I can remember, Benny never actually worked on the docks. He'd been on what's now called Workers' Compensation for years, even when I was a kid. When I was a kid, he'd often come to our house wearing a neck brace. When he arrived, he took the neck brace off.

"This thing is so uncomfortable," Benny said to my mother, visiting our house one time, placing the neck brace on the table.

"You're crazy, you know that?" my mother replied, laughing. My mother loved Benny, but she would never scheme the way he did; she did things the straight and narrow way. She worked and saved.

"But but, I have to be crazy to do this," said Benny, crushing his cigarette in the ashtray. He wore short-sleeve shirts, even in the winter. The bottom half of the shirt was light brown, the top half was dark brown with a stripe in the middle. This was the fashion in those days for Southern Italians in New York City.

"But but, I think they follow me around" said Benny, looking out of the window of our apartment. Benny's eyes were brilliantly blue. Their blueness shined brighter because of his dark hair and olive complexion. His head was long and rectangular, like it would fit perfectly in a gigantic boot box.

"Who follows you around?" asked my mother.

"The union insurance investigators," he said.

"The *what?*"

"Do you think they're going to let me collect workman's compensation without tracking me?"

My mother looked at my father, who was now doubling over with laughter.

"He's got to be careful," my father said, as if confirming Benny's reasoning. Yet, I'm not sure if my father believed that there were investigators flying around in helicopters, in cars and hiding behind doors, tracking Benny's movements. I'd never heard Benny once say that perhaps he was being followed because he hung out at the Ravenite.

But he was always calculating, working an angle. Always talking about schemes, how he could manipulate a situation.

One time he told us about how he avoided paying his dentist for the work he'd done on his wife, Accursia.

"Accursia had the work done; we couldn't pay it. But the doctor's office kept calling," he said. "But but, finally, after a few months, I picked up the phone and was surprised to hear the doctor himself calling," he added. Benny batted the smoke away from his face as he spoke. "You do realize that you're now nine months past due," says the doctor. After a pause, sighing, I says to the doctor, 'Look, I hate to tell you this, but my wife died.' The doctor was silent for a few seconds. The doctor then said he was sorry. I tried to sound like I was sad so the doctor would believe me," said Benny. "I must have done a good job because the doctor seemed to be convinced. The doctor said that Accursia was a beautiful person. And I said yes, we all loved her. I don't know what came over me, but I also said that he did a great job on her teeth. That she looked so pretty. We agreed that it was a shame such terrific work would go unappreciated by the world. Then I started to cry."

Saying that his wife died to avoid paying a bill didn't sound too horrible. So, the dentist would be out a few thousand dollars.

The closest Benny came to bragging was his talking about John Gotti. He called him John.

"But but, I got this watch from John," he said once, showing us his Rolex. I imagined it was stolen off a truck and was given to Benny for his service, or for a holiday. I never asked.

When he invited our family to his daughter's wedding at Russo's On The Bay, Benny said that he would have a special closed-off room for Gotti's family.

"He doesn't want to talk to nobody," said Benny. This was during the time when Gotti was under intense surveillance and investigation. I didn't know it at the time, but the FBI was trying every way to eavesdrop on Gotti's phone calls. They tapped his car, they bugged staircases and bathrooms in the Ravenite. By tracking his every movement, noticing Gotti would disappear for a few hours every day, the FBI finally discovered that Gotti and his crew escaped to an apartment near the Ravenite. The room had been owned by an old woman who died and somehow ownership was transferred to one of Gotti's associates. It was in this room, thinking that they were undetected, that Gotti and his crew spoke openly of murders and other crimes. Because of these recordings, Gotti was indicted and would eventually die in jail.

The day of Benny's daughter's wedding, I was curious to meet Gotti.

"Is he there?" I asked my father. My father said he didn't know.

When Benny came over to our table, he pointed to the room in the back with the glass door and curtains.

"But but, that's where they'll be. He says he's going to come," said Benny. "He already gave the wedding present," added Benny, shaking his hand like he dropped a hot potato.

I don't think Gotti ever came to the wedding, though I'll never know for sure. While we were dancing the tarantella, the FBI might have been circling in helicopters or hiding in the bathroom stalls.

When my father was sick, Benny was at our family's side. He was kind and caring to my mother. I knew his heart was broken when my father died. I could see it in his eyes.

Many years later, like so many of my parents' family, Benny was diagnosed with cancer. I went down to the Cherry Street projects, a few blocks from the Ravenite, where he lived, to visit him.

Benny's hair had whitened, he looked skinny. While I was there, he fell asleep sitting on the couch. I stayed for a while talking to Accursia and my cousins. We knew what was coming.

The last time I saw Benny, I was shocked when Accursia walked me into their bedroom. Benny was lying down on the bed, shivering. His body was stiff, his hands trembling, but locked at his sides. His eyes were staring at the ceiling. He looked like the images of Nosferatu from the silent films. Accursia was calm, comforting him by stroking his forehead. She had grown accustomed to how terrible he looked. But I could have fainted at that moment. I had seen family members in the last stages of cancer, but there was something different about this. The catatonic state he was in and his quaking body had shaken me.

I left their apartment and walked up Mulberry Street. It was the end of summer. The San Gennaro festival lights hung from the lampposts. A perfect summer night, but it felt like the world was sinking into a hole and would vanish.

I didn't want to go home. I stopped in to say hello to my friend Ernie at E. Rossi & Company, on Grand and Mulberry. When I was a kid, I worked as a busboy during the San Gennaro Feast at Ferrara

Bakery & Cafe, a few stores down from E. Rossi. Benny and Accursia would come by to see me as I hustled tables.

Ernie and I talked about how Little Italy is disappearing. I told him that my godfather, Benny, was dying of cancer. That he probably only had a few days left.

"After all of the old-timers are gone, there won't be a Little Italy no more," said Ernie.

With Chinatown moving up and Soho moving down, all that remains of Little Italy is a few stores. Most of the original owners have sold the businesses to investors cashing in on the idea of Little Italy. The tourists still pour in from all over the world to have a cappuccino in an authentic Italian café.

When Benny, the Short Long Man, died a few days later, Little Italy shrunk just a little more.

22

In Sicily Some Barbers Also Pulled Teeth

I've been going to Vincent's Barber Shop on Cortelyou Road in Brooklyn since I moved to the Ditmas Park area in 2003.

Until recently, there has always been a packed crowd waiting for haircuts and shaves.

And now, since COVID, when I walk into the shop, I wear a mask. Everyone who enters the shop has to wear a mask, especially while getting a haircut. And when you're in the barber's chair, you're covered in plastic. And each station is separated by plexiglass dividers.

Today there are a few people ahead of me. I sit down to wait my turn.

When I first started going to Vincent's Barber Shop, what got me hooked was that I could not only get an excellent haircut, but I could practice my not-so-great Sicilian. Vincent and his son Vinny speak Sicilian the way my grandparents did. Like many Americans, my grandparents only spoke Sicilian to talk to each other, so whatever I learned, I learned by listening closely and asking questions.

Interestingly, Angelo, one of the other barbers, also from Sicily, often doesn't understand my Sicilian. Of course, this makes me feel even more self-conscious than I already do about how poorly I speak the language.

"You're close, you just have to work on your diction," says Vinny, the owner's son, trying to make me feel better. "OK, *veni cà*, come sit in the chair," he adds.

Vinny and I sometimes speak Sicilian, mostly in single words or phrases, as opposed to full sentences, to communicate something we don't want the other customers to hear. We jokingly use expressions like *maleducati* (rude) or *sfacimm* (bad person). Before Vinny's father, Vincent, passed away in 2018, he and I also had similar "conversations" in Sicilian. Vincent was a very gentle and nice man. He gave my youngest son his first haircut. My wife and I even videotaped it.

Originally from Catania, Sicily, Vincent came to New York in 1960. Vincent's father, Gaetano, and Vincent's grandfather were barbers back in Sicily.

Now sitting in the chair, looking in the mirror, I say, "My mother says that her grandfather from Sicily was a barber and that he also performed some basic medical procedures. Did your grandfather do the same thing?"

"He pulled teeth," says Vinny, laughing.

"My mother says that her grandfather did other things, too. Like removing moles."

"Barbers knew how to use sharp instruments, like scissors and razors. And if you lived in a small village and needed to have something lanced, a tooth removed, you couldn't wait for a doctor."

"That makes sense," I say.

"What do you want today?" asks Vinny, looking back at me in the mirror.

"Today I just want a trim. Let's do *La Grande Cosa* next week." By *La Grande Cosa* I mean my once-a-month bigger haircut. Sometimes the distinction between *La Grande Cosa* and a trim is slight. Being a good barber is about giving people what they ask for, even if what they ask for doesn't really make sense.

More than just getting a trim today, I'm asking Vinny about the history of the shop.

Vinny tells me that his father came to the United States with an arranged job and a place to live.

"In those days, paisans from the same town in Sicily would help you come over to the States."

"Did he work in Brooklyn?"

"No, first he worked in Manhattan. But, working for the union, they sent him to work on Saturdays in the shop we're in today."

"There was a barbers' union? I didn't know that."

"There used to be, but no longer."

"Is that when he bought the shop?"

"No, he worked in the shop, then that owner sold the shop. Ironically, a friend that he knew bought the shop from him years later."

"So, your father worked here before he bought the shop?" I ask.

"Yes, then the guy wanted to retire," says Vinny.

"Was it expensive to buy?"

"Not in those days. He sold my father the chairs," pointing to the chairs still in the shop, "sold him equipment, and signed the lease over to him."

"Man, life was different in those days," I say. "You've told me you have brothers. Why did you decide to become a barber?"

"I didn't want to go to college like my brothers," replies Vinny, chuckling. "I didn't know what I wanted to do."

"Do you think you'll retire from here?"

"No," he says emphatically. "First of all, the business has been impacted by COVID. Secondly, if the current landlord sells the building, the new person might raise the rent and kick me out."

"What do you think you'll do?"

"I'll figure that out when the time comes. I have two boys to put through school, so I'll have to do something. But for now, I'll be a barber, like my father was, his father and his father before him."

23

And Now We Can Sing

My grandparents and parents never talked about prejudice against Italians, although they certainly encountered it. Like many Southern Italian immigrants who fled death and starvation in an Italy that had abandoned them, they too found prosperity in America. They worked as laborers and in factories in their newly adopted country. In America, Italians like my grandparents could build productive lives, make a future for their children. Southern Italian immigrants were a largely uneducated population. Having left Italy in poverty, they arrived with only their bodies to work. They didn't talk or write about their experiences. They mostly remained silent.

Both of my grandparents on my mother's side were born in the United States. Both were Sicilian. My grandmother Carmela (Millie) worked in a book bindery most of her adult life. You don't often see someone like Millie portrayed in films. She was soft spoken, wise and forgiving. My grandfather Alberto, whose sister was born in Sicily, dropped out of school and then worked on the railroad until he retired. He'd been a laborer, digging trenches, tunneling through the catacombs of New York City. He then worked his way up to New York City train conductor. Alberto Alberti was built like a boxer, wiry and firm. His nose was thin and fine. He was handsome. And he was dark skinned; he looked Egyptian or Moroccan. He said that when he was younger, he wasn't allowed in certain bars because sometimes people said he was Black.

My grandparents were an immigrant family in transition. They lived amongst other Sicilians, some who were born in Italy and some who were born in the United States. They both spoke Sicilian. In the Lower East Side tenements where they lived, Sicilian and other Southern-Italian dialects were spoken along with Russian, Yiddish, Polish and German.

Some say Sicilian is a dialect and some say it's a different language. There are many words and expressions of Arabic origin in Sicilian. The Sicilian language also drifted from Italian due to Sicily's historical poverty and physical separation from the mainland. Core Sicilian words like *patri* (father) and *bedda* (beautiful) are different than in standard Italian. Interestingly, there is no future tense in the Sicilian language.

My grandparents didn't teach us Sicilian; they only spoke it so we wouldn't understand them. It was a secret language. My grandparents, like many immigrants, tried to maintain their difference in a private manner. They didn't trust outsiders anyway. Why waste time explaining yourself when you couldn't really trust people who were not your family? Explaining yourself to others seemed like an esoteric task. Focus on the things you have control over, I can hear them say. Don't worry about these things, work hard, save your money.

When I was sick, I stayed at my grandparents' house. They were both retired. My parents worked. They knew it was time for me to go home when I became restless.

As I would get ready to leave, my grandmother would say to my grandfather "*dacci 'na cosa.*" It meant "give him something." My grandfather reached for a few dollars from the porcelain leaf ashtray, stacked with change and dollar bills, which sat on the radiator. I knew what it meant because I had heard it many times. My grandmother would say, "It's our dialect, you won't understand it," as if the Sicilian language defied translation. And perhaps Sicilian, like the stone caves in north-central Sicily, was impenetrable, its rough-hewn exterior protecting a soft fleshy interior.

Years later in high school, then in college, I studied Italian. We were taught that it was the Florentine dialect, the language of Dante. A language connected by antiquity to Caesar, Cicero and Lucretius. The language that nourished the Western world. The tongue my grandparents spoke was the language of poor immigrants, and of book bindery and railroad workers. There was a swallowed shame in speaking Sicilian.

My parents didn't speak Italian or Sicilian at all, though they knew some words and phrases. When my parents were children between the two world wars, many Italians, especially Southerners, concealed their foreignness. They only spoke the language amongst each other and never in public. In secret. Even some of the novelty songs of their era belie the Southern Italian tendency for dual expression: one private and one public. For example, the English lyrics for "Zooma Zooma," a song by Louis Prima, are silly and nonsensical, but the dialect translations of the verses are risqué and suggestive. There was power in keeping it hidden. They knew what it really meant, and you didn't.

As I studied Italian, I'd try to speak it to my grandparents. When my grandfather said things like "*Mancia cava*" meaning "you eat like a horse," I just stared at him blankly. Sentences were condensed. Entire portions of words were lopped off for brevity. He'd make fun of me, calling me "Il Professore" since I was only book learned. In fact, growing up in New York City, I heard mostly Southern Italian dialects. I was hardly ever able to use the Italian I was studying though I could read and write it with some facility. Then, one summer in college, while working at the Berkshire Hotel on Madison Avenue in Manhattan, I overheard Italians speaking. I was told that they were from the magazine *L'Uomo*, preparing for a fashion show. From Milan. As if my ears were suddenly activated, I was startled to discover that I could understand what they were saying. First just the words, then the sentences. It was a miraculous experience. I hid behind a curtain and listened as if I had been deaf all my life and could now hear.

Imagine hearing a language all of your life that you can't understand. Imagine privately experiencing a culture all of your life that is perceived and portrayed very differently in the public eye.

When I was about ten, I gave my grandfather a plain Hallmark card for his birthday. When you opened it, it read "You're the best grandpa ever." I signed it "I love you" and drew hearts on it. This man, who was tough as nails, read the card and started crying, wiping the tears from his eyes. He then got on his knees to get at my level and hugged me. As resilient as he was all of his life, for his family, he was defenseless in that moment. I didn't understand why he cried. Seeing him break down for a moment was like watching a door to his soul burst open.

This is a very Sicilian and in general a very Southern Italian predicament. Since the time of Shakespeare up until the present day, we've been portrayed as tough clowns. Sometimes we're the Mafia killer with dark pockmarked skin, greasy hair and fancy clothes. Sometimes we're depicted as the cold-blooded capo. Despite the fact that he talks like he has rocks in his mouth, the cold-blooded capo dresses well and is ruthlessly cunning. Sometimes the tough clown is a loud wife, cooking in the kitchen, threatening her children with cooking utensils, "Wait until your father comes home, you little sons a bitches." And we're supposed to laugh at ourselves along with other people laughing at our expense.

People still laugh or trivialize. I'm still surprised when I have to defend the fact that there is prejudice against Italians. I'm especially surprised when I have to defend this fact even to my liberal friends. Sympathy for Italian Americans is an outlier phenomenon. Let me explain.

About two years ago, I worked for a large organization. As with any large organization, I worked with people from all over the globe. And like all employees, I had to take compulsory cultural sensitivity training. It's easy to miss a cue or lack understanding due to cultural differences. After all, most of the employees had a business or technical background and didn't study anthropology, history or other liberal-arts subjects.

One time, I walked into a meeting room in New York City surrounded by a table of people from all over the world: India, China, Russia, Ethiopia, France, and from all over the United States.

As I walked into the room, I was greeted by the Director of North East.

"Hey, oh, yo Mikey," he said. "How you doin'?" he added, imitating Italian American movie speech. His salutation was met by a flurry of chuckles.

I have to admit internally I was shocked. Externally, having experienced this many times over, I did what I've always done, what my grandparents and parents had done, what most Italian Americans still do. I ignored it. It wasn't so much that I was insulted, it was more of the fact that a high-level director with dozens of reports felt it was OK to do this in front of a room of international peers. Why didn't I report him to human resources right away? I had a room full of witnesses. Keep your mouth shut, do your job.

As Italians, we are taught to accept this kind of behavior in our workplace, amongst friends and even amongst people we've just met. Even from people with master's degrees, from educated backgrounds. And why not? There are countless movies and television shows depicting Italian clown tough guys with rough ugly faces who spit when they speak. As if the industry would entertain other stories or portrayals, they instead shuck off accusations of bias saying many of the shows and films are written by Italian writers and filmmakers.

I'm OK with Mafia films. I'm OK with portrayals of tough-guy clowns. They exist. Show them. But now it's time to write our own stories. Stories that also depict Italian Americans as regular Americans and as regular people. Stories about the great Italian American jazz players. Stories about the Italian bel-canto singing style—from Caruso to Sinatra—that launched American music worldwide. Stories about your uncle who was a gifted piano player.

The curious dismissal of Italian American prejudice is as much a mystery now as it was in the time of my grandparents. Until we are vigilant in our watch against all prejudice, until we listen to each other and sing our own stories aloud, racism will persist for all.

About the Author

Mike Fiorito is currently an Associate Editor for Mad Swirl Magazine and a regular contributor to the Red Hook Star Revue. In 2019, he was nominated for the Pushcart Prize by Ovunque Siamo Press.

Mike is the author four books; *Freud's Haberdashery Habits* (Alien Buddha Press, 2018), *Hallucinating Huxley* (Alien Buddha Press, 2018), *Call Me Guido* (Ovunque Siamo Press, 2019), and *Falling from Trees* (Loyola College/Apprentice House, 2021). He was also a contributor to *A Feast of Narrative: An Anthology of Short Stories By Italian American Writers*, (Volume I and Volume III).

In *Sleeping with Fishes*, Fiorito says: "I write about my family be-cause it's hard to write about...and because it matters." He takes on the hard job, and it does matter. He breaks the Italian code of silence. He writes about real people. What a joy. No more stereotypes, no more cli-chés. From sacred to profane, Italians are not all about pizza, Hollywood movies and Mafia, folks. Fiorito's insights into his Sicilian American family of origin are riveting. The last chapter is a masterpiece.

— SUSAN CAPERNA LLOYD
No Pictures in My Grave: A Spiritual Journey in Sicily

Mike Fiorito's *Sleeping with Fishes* is the essence of Italianità, but you don't have to be Italian to appreciate the essays in this funny and touching collection. Here, Fiorito's journalistic chops show us how authentic cannoli are made but also how to bridge the yawning gap between the Italian he learns at school and the Sicilian dialect of his immigrant grandparents. Fiorito makes the connections real, and this is a delightful read.

— MARIANNE LEONE
MA SPEAKS UP (BeaconPress)

Two decades ago, Gay Talese asked where the Italian American storytellers were, blaming our hesitancy to tell our stories on the strictures of omertà. "What happens in the family stays in the family" was our 11th Commandment, inbred in Italians--especially in Sicilians--long before Las Vegas was born. Bravo once more to Mike Fiorito, whose latest collection of family laundry, *Sleeping with Fishes*, sparkles on the clothesline, waving in the sun and fresh air, billowing and free. With wit, wisdom, honesty and questions, Fiorito unabashedly shares his family history with us and we are better for it. I eagerly await the contents of Fiorito's next laundry basket.

— KAREN TINTORI
UNTO THE DAUGHTERS: The Legacy of an Honor Killing in a Sicilian-American Family

Sleeping with Fishes dances to the heartbeat of the Sicilian American soul, its complications, its longings, and its secrets. Another wonderful read by Fiorito, packed full of canny wit and verve.

— CHRISTINA MARROCCO
Associate Professor of English, Elgin Community College

Made in the USA
Las Vegas, NV
28 August 2021